About Muhammad

About Muhammad

THE OTHER WESTERN PERSPECTIVE ON THE PROPHET OF ISLAM

A SHORT ANTHOLOGY OF WESTERN WRITINGS
ON THE PROPHET MUHAMMAD: FROM THE
18TH CENTURY TO THE PRESENT

Edited with an Introduction by
ABDELWAHAB EL-AFFENDI

LEGACY
PUBLISHING

Legacy Publishing Ltd
P.O. Box 782,
Richmond, Surrey, TW9 2WA, UK
www.legacy-publishing.com

ISBN 978-0-9557463-9-0 PAPERBACK
ISBN 978-0-9557463-8-3 HARDBACK

*The views and opinions expressed in this book are the contributors
and not necessarily those of the publisher.*

Typesetting and cover design by Sideek Ali
Printed and bound in Malta by Gutenberg Press Ltd

Contents

Mahomet was in his fortieth year, when having withdrawn to a cavern in Mount Hara, near Mecca... he one day told his wife Kadijah... That by the unspeakable special favor of Heaven he had now found it all out; was in doubt and darkness no longer, but saw it all. That all these Idols and Formulas were nothing, miserable bits of wood; that there was One God in and over all... That God is great; and that there is nothing else great! He is the Reality. – and then also "Islam," That we must submit to God. That our whole strength lies in resigned submission to Him... – "If this be Islam," says Goethe, "do we not all live in Islam?" Yes, all of us that have any moral life; we all live so.

Thomas Carlyle
On Heroes, Hero-Worship and the Heroic in History (1888)

PUBLISHER'S NOTE

The Reader is advised that in order to preserve this collection of essays, the original spelling and grammar has been retained. The different spelling of the name 'Muhammad' has also been retained as in the original texts; together with the original referencing and citation style, rather than being standardised to the Publisher's house style.

Legacy Publishing Ltd
London, August 2010 – Ramadan, 1431 AH

Foreword

MUCH has been written about European hostility towards Muslims and their faith, and, indeed, much of that hostility has been and is directed at their Prophet. Indeed many today are tempted to affirm an anachronistic idea of eternal hostility between Islam and the West. Normal Daniel has argued that powerful and hostile medieval stereotypes of Islam and its founder, based on Christian doctrinal unity and opposition to Islam, were robust enough to survive the failure of the Crusades, the rise of Protestantism, the Enlightenment, atheism and scepticism. Indeed, as El-Affendi notes in his Introduction, such medieval attitudes appear to be alive and well today.

But such medieval views of the Prophet did not survive the last few centuries wholly intact either. As this small selection of more sympathetic voices indicates, alternative views were and have been on offer. Yet due care should be taken in reading these extracts too. The temptation is to read them simply on a scale of greater or lesser fidelity to the orthodox Muslim representation of the Prophet's life, but this pious impulse, while understandable, will not help us to understand these texts fully.

All these texts build upon the emergence of historical scholarship based on primary Arabic and other sources that appeared in the seventeenth century in Europe. To a greater or lesser extent all these extracts are concerned to move away from the medieval idea of the

Prophet as an insincere imposter, mostly notably after the contribution of Thomas Carlyle (1795–1881), the Scottish essayist and satirist, who viewed this as historically incomprehensible in case of the Prophet. His 1840 essay on the hero as prophet was influential enough to undermine this as a meaningful or useful question among serious scholars of the Prophet's life.

Another trend is a shifting away from overt to more implicit or even sublimated Christian missionary impulses. George Sale (c. 1697–1736), whose English translation of the Qur'an was published in 1734, was better disposed towards the Prophet than many of his contemporaries. His long introduction, which contained a brief account of the Prophet's life, was published separately and was translated into other languages; it influenced, among others, Voltaire. Yet Sale's concern for greater accuracy and even sympathy was clearly driven by the need to inform Protestant mission and to prove the superiority of Protestantism at the same time. Even among some of much more professional and rigorous historians who make up the selection from the twentieth century, such as the late Reverend Montgomery Watt (1909–2006), one of the most prolific British scholars of Islam, a propensity to compare Islam to a Christian norm is noticeable.

In the selection of texts here from the latter half of the twentieth century, even sublimated Christian mission falls away to be replaced by a phenomenological approach, in which the overriding concern is to present Islam as Muslims themselves see it, and to bracket one's own private judgements as far as possible. Yet all these writers are concerned to rebut unfair or hostile stereotypes of Islam and its founder, even if questions of truth do not ultimately enter into their descriptive exercise.

A final point perhaps is to ask whether it is still meaningful to talk of "the West" in opposition to Islam in at least one very important sense. The twentieth century, particularly in its latter stages, saw the emergence of serious Islamic scholarship in European languages, written by Muslims in and of the West. To take one prominent example, Martin Lings' (1909–2005) biography *Muhammad* (1983) received wide acclaim in the Muslim world and prizes from the governments of Egypt and Pakistan. We ought therefore to be cognizant of the inherent danger of perpetuating Islam and the West as mutually constitutive and exclusive categories for in so doing we may be furthering the very polarity that we wish to put an end to.

Yahya Birt
Leicester, April 2010

Preface

WHEN Pope Benedict XVI stirred a huge controversy in September 2006 by his remarks reiterating old Christian accusations against the Prophet Muhammad of having spread Islam by violence, what was most remarkable was that the Pope did not seem to think that he had said something outrageous. Pope Benedict XVI was giving a lecture at the University of Regensburg in Bavaria, when he quoted Byzantine Emperor Manuel II Palaiologos' exclamation: "Show me just what Mohammed brought that was new, and there you will find things only evil and inhuman, such as his command to spread by the sword the faith he preached." When Muslims the world over expressed near unanimous outrage at the remarks, the Pope and his supporters were completely unable to see the point. Even US Secretary of State Condoleezza Rice could not see it, remarking that "We all need to understand that offense can sometimes be taken when perhaps we don't see it."

The reason why the Pope or Rice could not see the offence made is due to the fact that Western culture has incorporated the abuse of Islam and the denigration of its Prophet as an integral part of European Western and cultural identity. As we will show below, Western polemics and propaganda against Islam and its Prophet are as old as Islam itself, and have coloured all discourse in Islam since then.

It is for this same reason that the offence made by Salman Rushdie's novel *The Satanic Verses* (1988) appeared also a mystery to most Western thinkers and policy makers. It was the same with the Danish Cartoons outrage, which erupted following the publication on 30 September 2005 of 12 cartoons ridiculing the Prophet Muhammad in the Danish newspaper Jyllands-Posten. Again the intense "irrational" anger of Muslims inside and outside Denmark appeared unfathomable to the Danish people and government and most Europeans. In all these cases, Western intellectuals and leaders wondered why Muslims were so angry, and defended the freedom of expression of those causing the offence.

While the Muslim side had probably overreacted in all these instances, the point is that the inability of Western opinion to appreciate the enormity of the offence (especially when it was the result of a deliberate and premeditated calculation as was the case with Rushdie) shows how deep the prejudices and misrepresentations invoked go within the Western psyche. It is to be noted that the Pope's lecture, entitled "Faith, Reason and the University," did not need to mention Islam. Its topic was the ongoing contest over European identity, with the Pope arguing that the blend of Biblical doctrine and Greek rationalism which characterized European Christianity should be celebrated and not deplored. He thus criticized both secular rationalists who wanted to do away with religion, and Christian purists who wanted to purge Christianity of "alien" Greek accretions. What the Pope was defending was in fact the Europeanness of Christianity rather than the Christianity of Europe. Since the Pope is known to oppose Turkey's accession to the EU in order to safeguard Europe's Christian identity, this angle appears to be an attempt to kill three birds with one stone: to insist on a role for religion in public life and oppose total secularization; to convince secular sceptics that Christianity is not only a defining feature of European identity, but has in fact been also defined by this identity; and to promote the "Christian" exclusivity of the European Union.

In this rush to claim both Christianity and rationality for Europe alone, the discourse the Pope has relied on neglected to refer to a rather embarrassing counterpoint. As one perceptive commentator put it, in his eagerness "to demonstrate the compatibility of the Christian faith with reason… as defined in classical Greek philosophy… regrettably, at the expense of Islam and Prophet Mohammed, reviving anti-Islamic prejudices of the Middle Ages," the Pope neglected one important detail.

> In his lecture preaching the compatibility of reason and faith, Benedict XVI, the scholar, deliberately overlooks the fact that the insights of Greek philosophy – its commitment to [reason] – have been brought to medieval Christian Europe by the great Muslim thinkers of the Middle Ages. What he calls the "encounter between the Biblical message and Greek thought" (Par. 5 of his lecture) was, to a large extent, the result of the influence of Muslim philosophers – at a time when European Christians were totally ignorant of classical Greek philosophy.[1]

This presumed encounter between Christianity and Greek rationality thus turns out to be in fact an encounter between Christianity and *Islamic* rationality, thus directly refuting his central claim that Islam has always been devoid of rationality and hostile to it.

In this respect, the Western discourse about Islam, as symbolized by the distorted narratives about Prophet Muhammad's life and teachings, tends to be an indirect discourse about the self: it is an attempt to define the elusive Western identity by a series of exclusions through comparison. At the start, the attacks on the Prophet were seen as an easy defensive strategy in order to defend Christian identity against what was seen as an existential threat to its political structure and religious identity. If you could discredit the Prophet, there is no need to enter into a serious theological discussion with the followers of Islam. This is, interestingly, the same strategy adopted by the Prophet's opponents in his own tribe of Quraysh, when they also argued among themselves about how to discredit him, and thought about calling him a madman, a poet, a seer, etc., and admitted than none of these would stick. So in the end they decided to call him a magician who bewitches people with his rhetoric. Interestingly, one can see the same agonising among some modern "Orientalist" authors, such as the Marxist French author Maxime Rodinson, who also admits that the Prophet cannot be convincingly labelled a liar or a fraud, and ended up arguing that the Quran was the product of the Prophet's own "unconscious." After considering and dismissing accounts such as Voltaire's and Grimme's which accept that the Prophet made up the message for noble purposes (to raise the Arabs to glory or help the poor), Rodinson uses the Freudian concept of the "unconscious" in order to explain why Muhammad could be seen both as sincere but deluded at the same time.[2]

While Rodinson's account, in spite of its avowed atheist perspective, is considered to be relatively more balanced than that of many rivals, for even after Christianity started to wane, secular intellectuals, poets, novelists, etc. from the Renaissance through the Enlightenment continued to attack Islam and its Prophet, this time in the name of civilization and rationality. With the rise of colonialism and the decisive secularization of the West, Orientalism took the mantle of defending the West and advancing its interests, this time in the guise of "objective" knowledge. Instead of attacking Muhammad as an impostor and "Anti-Christ," now "scientific" arguments were marshalled to explain how his delusions had arisen and were accepted, and at times even to question his historical existence. As Orientalism began to be discredited, some new voices have arisen which attempted to revive the old prejudices and stoke the flames of hostility.

However, at all these stages, a number of sober voices have courageously dissented from the general view and did not swallow the official propaganda hook, line and sinker. During the earlier periods, this was a dangerous endeavour, and those who dared speak out were severely attacked and often silenced. Many had to circulate their views anonymously for fear of persecution. Later, however, the dissenting voices became more frequent and more open.

In what follows, we present a small selection of views that tried to give a more considered view of the life of the Prophet of Islam. Being the writings of people who were non-Muslim by definition, many still regarded the Prophet's message with scepticism. However, they have eschewed the crude propagandist attacks of other authors and tried to offer a more balanced and more historically accurate view.

It is our hope that presenting this selection will help further the dialogue between the adherents of Islam and other faiths by showing

Preface

Muslims that not all Westerners harbour implacable hostility to Islam, and by offering others a different perspective on the life of the man who is still the "most talked-of person in the whole range of human history," as one author recently put it.[3]

Abdelwahab El-Affendi
London, February 2010

Introduction

WHEN the Prophet Muhammad declared his mission in Arabia, the Christian West, consumed by its own internal political and religious struggles, hardly paid any attention to the event.[1] However, even before the rise of Islam, the Arabs were viewed through a prism of combined religious-racial prejudice in Christian intellectual circles as evidenced by this statement by Archbishop Isidore of Seville (c. 560–636):

> The Saracens live in the desert. They are also called the Ishmaelites, as the book of Genesis teaches, because they are descended from Ishmael. They are also called Hagarenes because they are descended from Hagar. They also, as we have already said, perversely call themselves Saracens because they mendaciously boast of descent from Sarah.[2]

These remarks by a prominent religious figure and historians (who was a contemporary of the Prophet), and the false accusation to the Arabs of claiming descent from Sarah, clothe racial prejudice into religious garb by repeating a slur (endorsed even by modern commentators, including the source from which we cited this quote) against the Prophet Abraham in branding his marriage to Hagar as "illegitimate" (and insinuating that Ishmael therefore was an illegitimate child!). According to this claim, descent from Hagar does not qualify the Arabs as legitimate descendants of Abraham. This made it easier later to transfer this prejudice against the "Saracens" to cover their religion.

However, if the Christians in the distant West could afford indifference vis-à-vis the rise of Islam, their Byzantine rivals with whom they were locked into a mortal combat did not feel the same way. The Byzantine and their Ghassanide vassals in Syria did not only take note, but moved actively to try to contain the new religion, leading to the famous confrontations in Mu'ata and Tabuk. It is interesting that these early confrontations became in themselves the fodder of later polemics that continued into modern times in Orientalist discourse, with claims and counter-claims about who started the military confrontations and on what motives.[3]

While those early battles were a trigger, the lightning progress of Muslim armies through Byzantine possessions in Syria, Egypt and North Africa (and the later move into Catholic Spain) were a traumatic experience that posed more than a military challenge to Christendom. It was also a serious spiritual and intellectual challenge requiring "an urgent answer to the mystery of Islam's position in relationship to Christianity."

> Was Islam a heresy, a schism? Was it a parody of Christianity or a new religion, a separate school of thought which deserved respect and recognition? Or was it a joint work of Man and Devil? These were the anguished questions which medieval Christians asked themselves and which, in various guises, have continued to agonize Christian commentators and Western writers down to our own century. Why were Muslims so impervious to the appeal of Christianity, when their Qur'an recognized Jesus as Messiah? There were those who hoped that it was indeed a sect, a branch of the Church, which needed enlightenment. But for centuries, attempts to baptize these stray sheep failed, a source of great anxiety and distress to many who then became bitter opponents of Islam, condemning it to literal damnation.[4]

In the same way that Muhammad's opponents within his tribe were bewildered by his call and had to resort to defamation against his person in order to find an easy way out, Medieval Europe decided to take the same course of action:

Introduction

Medieval scholars and churchmen preferred to give the easy answer to the question of what was Islam: that it was the work of one man, Muhammad, and that he was inspired by Satan. There was thus no need to answer awkward questions about the religion; defame its founder and you could forget the rest. Fantastic legends and fables began to emerge in order to frighten Christians away from the dreadful possibility of conversion to the other religion. It was asserted, for instance, that Muhammad had died not in the year 632 CE but in 666 – the number of the Beast in the Apocalypse, so he must be the Anti-Christ. With his name corrupted to 'Mahound,' Muhammad became the 'Devil incarnate.'[5]

The campaign started early. A Christian tract which appeared at around 638 CE/16 AH, contains this comment ascribed to a Palestinian Jew:

A false prophet has appeared among the Saracens ... They say that the prophet has appeared coming with the Saracens, and is proclaiming the advent of the anointed one who is to come. I, Abraham, referred the matter to an old man very well-versed in the scriptures. I asked him: 'What is your view, master and teacher, of the prophet who has appeared among the Saracens?' He replied, groaning mightily: 'He is an impostor. Do the prophets come with sword and chariot? Truly these happenings today are works of disorder ... But you go off, Master Abraham, and find out about the prophet who has appeared.' So I, Abraham, made enquiries, and was told by those who had met him: 'There is no truth to be found in the so-called prophet, only bloodshed; for he says he has the keys of paradise, which is incredible.'[6]

The campaign continued throughout medieval times, taking a direct polemical form. It became in fact constitutive of European identity, as hatred and fear of Islam were used by religious leaders as the cement to unite the warring Europeans. As one commentator put it, "Indeed, it can be reasonably argued that Christian self-identity was forged in part by its sense that it was always on the verge of being overwhelmed by the 'other' of Islam."[7] Attacks on the Prophet became the key to this. "The demonization of the prophet... was to become the very instrument of the making of Christian Europe. Psychologically and physically Islam was regarded as Christianity's worst enemy, threatening Christian identity and its very sense of superiority. The Crusades, which extended from 1095 to 1270, were only one expression of this great Christian resurgence."[8]

However, even at that early stage, there were some dissenting voices. Peter the Venerable, Abbot of Cluny, criticized the Crusades in 1142 as ineffective and too violent, arguing that peaceful engagement with Islam would help the Christian cause better. While still championing a determined campaign against Islam, which he described as "the error of errors," he was more in favour of preaching, and was credited with setting up an embryonic "Orientalist" project by organizing translations of Arabic works.[9] Writing in the 13th Century, the English Philosopher Roger Bacon (1214/1220–1292), refuted some of the myths Christian entertained about Muhammad as the Anti-Christ and argued that Islam was gaining more success than Christianity and had to be dealt with peacefully and rationally.[10] Bacon, who had read the works of leading Muslim philosophers in Latin and was influenced by them, was described by Muhammad Iqbal as "one of the apostles of Muslim science and method."[11] He advocated what another author called a "scientific crusade," which championed the cause of the Crusades of achieving world dominance for the Roman church, but in a more subtle way under the banner of "universal peace."[12]

In the 15th Century, Bishop John of Segovia in Spain (d. 1458) suggested to fellow bishops the need to translate the Quran in order to better understand Islam and reconcile it with Christianity. His translation of the Quran disappeared, but his commentary on it survived. One of his collaborators, the Italian Aenas Silvius, who became Pope in 1458, sent a message to Sultan Muhammad II (the Conqueror) urging him not to underestimate European strength because he had conquered Constantinople, and inviting him to embrace Christianity and promising to make him Emperor of Europe if he did. In his letter he writes:

There are many points of agreement between Christians and Muslims; One God, the Creator of the World, a belief in the necessity for faith, a future life of rewards and punishment, the immortality of soul and the common use of the Old Testament as a basis. All this is shared grounds. We only differ about the nature of God.[13]

However, these (relatively) conciliatory remarks remained isolated, in spite of the relative openness brought about by the Renaissance and the later Enlightenment. While the Crusades and their fanatical anti-Muslim rhetoric have set the stage for unrestrained invective against Islam and its prophet, one of the early "scholarly" contributions which stand out in this campaign was the book by Humphrey Prideaux (1648–1724), an English priest and scholar, whose intensely polemical 1697 work *The True Nature of Imposture Fully Displayed in the Life of Mahomet* became one of the most influential sources of knowledge about the Prophet.[14]

Nevertheless, even during this period of rising intolerance, a few voices arose which tried to defy the prevailing unremitting and uninformed prejudice. But precisely for this reason, most of these commentators had to hide their identity. One courageous voice who was unafraid to declare himself in public was the British George Sale (1697–1736) who produced one of the first English translations of the Quran (1734). He prefaced his work with a commentary including a short biography of the Prophet. Sale endured severe attacks for his mildly sympathetic comments about the Prophet, and had to be defended many years later against the charge of having put Islam on equal footing with Christianity.[15]

Viscount Henry Bolingbroke (1678–1751), a prominent British politician, also made an important contribution to this effort, criticizing in his *Letters on the Study of the Use of History* (1735) the fanatical and unjustified attacks against Islam by the Christian establishment. He reminded his audience that the common accusations against Muslims of being idolaters were made by people more worthy of such accusations (see extract below). In 1728, the French historian Henri de Boulainvilliers, Count of Saint-Saire (1658–1722) published *La Vie de Mahomet*, described by a recent publisher as "one of the most fascinating accounts of the life of the Prophet to be written that early in the west," and by one commentator as "the eighteenth century's most sympathetic account of Islam."[16] Although he still calls Muhammad "an imposter," he describes him as "an enlightened and wise lawgiver," who "was neither coarse nor barbarous; [...] he conducted his enterprise with all the art, all the delicacy, all the resolution, all the intrepidity and extensive views that Alexander or Caesar had been capable of, in his circumstances."[17]

A more radical anonymous author, believed to be the Oxford librarian Henry Stubbe (1632–1676), wrote a work entitled: *An Account of the Rise and Progress of Mahometanism with the Life of Mahomet and a Vindication of Him and His Religion from the Calumnies of the Christians.* Given the provocative title, the manuscript was circulated privately and only became publicly known after the author's death. It was officially published only in 1911, but some analysts suggest that Prideaux's attack on the Prophet was most probably a response to Stubbe's anonymous work.[18]

Stubbe's biography appeals for a reappraisal of the historical affinities between the 'Religions of the Book,' adopting a comparative approach to some extent implicit in contemporary travel narratives and religious treatises, but which is here transformed into a far-reaching religious syncretism... Stubbe offers a portrait of Mohammed as a shrewd politician without the customary accompanying condemnation. Instead, the 'Excellency of his Laws' derives directly from their pragmatism, and his ability to harness the natural religious inclination of humanity in the furtherance of empire is deemed positively praiseworthy. In this respect, Stubbe's explicit acclamation of the political and religious unity of the Islamic state – the union of 'the Civil and Ecclesiastical Powers in one Sovereign' – is Leviathan-like in its prescription, echoing a work that Stubbe undoubtedly admired... Stubbe does not refute the standard depiction of an empire driven by the sword, but makes a crucial distinction between religion and nation that signals an entirely new conception of Islam: 'It is manifest that the Mahometans did propagate their Empire, but not their Religion, by force of arms.' By pointed contrast, Christian princes seem bent upon the persecution of their own people in the name of religion. Rather, a degree of religious toleration is conducive to good empire-building as Stubbe maintains in a direct allusion to (his own) present-day Islam.[19]

Introduction

Again, these remained isolated, prudently anonymous voices. Even the more secular figures in European renaissance (including Shakespeare, Chaucer, Milton, Dante, Marlowe, etc.) perpetuated the theme of the Muslim ('Turk') as hate figure, a threat, the 'Other' or the enemy to be overcome by heroes.[20] With the Reformation, the theme of Muhammad as 'Anti-Christ' was revived again by Luther and other figures, and used to demonize the Pope and the institutional Catholic Church as being 'worse than Muhammad.'

The Enlightenment, which coincided during the 18th century with the receding of the Turkish threat to Europe and the rise of European self-confidence, brought no respite for Muslims. Key figures in the Enlightenment (such as Voltaire, Montesquieu, Kant, etc.) used attacks on the Prophet Muhammad and Islam as an indirect method of attacking the Church and the monarchy, but in the process contributed to exacerbating popular prejudice against Islam. While Montesquieu's *Persian Letters* (1725) was ambiguous in that it used the account of Persian life to satirize Louis XIV's France, as well as being disparaging of Muslim beliefs and practices, Voltaire's play *Le fanatisme, ou Mahomet le Prophete, (Fanaticism, or Mahomet the Prophet)* (1736) was a frontal attack on the Prophet of Islam. It portrays the Prophet as a cynical manipulator in pursuit of power and his own personal desires, while the pagan Meccans are shown as defendants of liberty and enemies of Muhammad's tyranny. Granted that Voltaire had ulterior motives, as for him, "the figure of the prophet served in this play to illuminate the tyranny and hypocrisy of the French clerical establishment."[21] However, some of his remarks suggests that however "enlightened" he may have been, he maintained an attitude identical to that of the early Crusader fanatics. Another leading figure in the Enlightenment, the German philosopher Immanuel Kant also joined the attack by describing the Prophet as one of the worst fanatics.[22]

The advance of the Enlightenment did not imply the decline of the crusading mentality. Voltaire, like many lesser but not necessarily less enlightened contemporaries, desired to annihilate the Turks. He held them, together with the plague, to be the greatest curse on earth. "It does not suffice to humiliate them," he said, "they should be destroyed." As his personal correspondence shows, he deeply regretted that "the Christian powers, instead of destroying the common enemy, are busy ruining each other."[23]

These are almost identical words to those used by Pope Urban II as he launched the Crusades in 1095!

However, the same could not be said about the more literary section of the Enlightenment. The German poet Johann Goethe (1749–1832) wrote a song called "Mahomet's Song" (1772) in which he "celebrates the pure, infinite, self-generating energy of the spirit within, embodied in the figure of Muhammad and his prophesy."[24] In his later years, Goethe embraced mystical themes from the Orient, and Islam in particular. Another poet, the French Alphonse Marie Louis de Lamartine (1790–1869), also wrote fondly of the Prophet as follows:

> By the 19th century, when the German philosopher Georg Wilhelm Friedrich Hegel (1770–1831) was giving a positive assessment of Islam's role in history, something fundamental appeared to have changed. By the middle of the nineteenth century, the traditional image of Muhammad as "anti-Christ" had become passé, and in the general framework of Victorian discussions of the Prophet has somewhat an air of quaint antediluvianism. Anti-Christ he may not have been, but the issue of his imposture remained crucial.[25]

The shift was symbolised by Thomas Carlyle's lecture on Muhammad, "The Hero as Prophet" as follows:

> Carlyle found in the inner experience of the Arabian prophet, that quintessential quality of his Great Men – sincerity. Carlyle's image of the Prophet as hero was both cause and effect of a significant shift in attitudes to Islam and its founder which occurred during the eighteenth and nineteenth centuries in Europe, a shift which in its most general terms may be characterised as one from Islam as a Christian heresy and Muhammad a fraud and charlatan, to Islam as an authentic expression of religion and its founder a man of sincerity and genuine piety.[26]

Introduction

It has to be said the bulk continued to regard the Prophet as an impostor, but due both to the progressive detachment from earlier Christian fanaticism, whose theses became increasingly untenable, and the fact that Islam was no longer seen as a threat, it became relatively easier to discuss Islam dispassionately, even though the new found detachment did not preclude looking down on it. In some quarters, the fear and loathing now turned to pity and disdain. Islam was no longer a threat, charging sword in hand, bent on overwhelming the civilised Christian West. Now it was a stagnant, miserable faith in the throes of terminal decline.

Islam's "decline and stagnation" had to be explained by citing its "rigid dogmatism," "fatalism," the tendency to blind imitation, deference to despotism, and even the ban on alcohol.[27] These are themes which came to inform the new discipline of Orientalism, an intellectual pursuit which presented itself as a "scientific" endeavour as opposed to the earlier religious-based polemics. However, the bulk of Orientalists continued to be missionaries, colonial officials or both at the same time. What Edward Said (1935–2003), former Columbia University's Professor of Comparative Literature, tried to do in his influential *Orientalism* (1978)[28] was to unmask the hidden power dimensions and inherent biases of this supposedly "detached" discipline. Unlike Voltaire who was open about his desire to kill Turks, or the abbé de Saint-Pierre (1658–1743) who made no secret of his dream of "the conquest of Turkey" which "will be a true crusade" making it possible to "step by step populate, discipline, Christianize, polish the entire habitable Earth,"[29] the new and old Orientalists feigned detachment from the worldly links of power. They merely spoke "about the clash of civilisations" and deplored "what went wrong" with the non-Western world.

The contest over Orientalism engages with some of the most fundamental questions of human existence and human knowledge and raises a host of important philosophical and epistemological questions. The crisis faced by Orientalism's tenuous claims to the status of a science is symptomatic of a deeper malaise infecting modern "scientific" discourse in general.

Introduction

> [A]s a species of Enlightenment discourse, orientalism has been a carrier of basic Western notions of the European self and the non-Western other which generated unfalsifiable propositions about the superiority of Europeans to non-Europeans. In this way, orientalists participated in the elaboration of modern European cultural identity.[30]

The Western experience is thus used as the only yardstick with which to measure other experiences.

> When modernity is employed as an outward gaze of the West… what it seeks to achieve has an exact identity with the missionary and supremacist instincts that were part and parcel of all earlier stages and phases of Western expansion and its physical and intellectual conquest of the Orient.[31]

This means also that the inbuilt prejudices of ages past are also built into the methodology and premises of the disciplines. When a typical Orientalist statement is made (e.g. Elie Kedourie's claim that "Democracy is alien to the mind-set of Islam"),[32] one accepts a host of assumptions and beliefs about "Islam," "the West," "democracy," religion, society, history, culture, civilization, and so forth which remain largely unexamined because they are taken for granted. It is the internal erosion of these certainties which have worked to undermine classical Orientalism. The developments leading to this included the decline of beliefs in the truth and superiority of Christianity, changes in perceptions about culture and civilization, changes in the function of scholarship, which was no longer required to serve state (or Church) policy directly, the proliferation of empirical research in other cultures and, no less significant, the challenge to the monopoly of traditional Orientalist scholarship both from within and from outside the West.

This crisis can also be seen as a reflection of the general crisis of the post-Enlightenment "state-centered liberal project" with its obsessive tendency "to quantify, map and control" and the implication that the "kind of sociology of Islam that emerged is shaped to the deeply problematic history of the encounter in the West between religion and the state."[33]

Introduction

Said's effective demolition of Orientalism marked a turning point similar to that brought about by the Enlightenment. Just as the Enlightenment made it untenable to circulate the same old myths and fairytales about Islam, the post-*Orientalism* world (which also coincided with the "post-modern" era and its critique of the Enlightenment and western modernity in general) made in untenable to circulate the same old Orientalist narratives which treats Muslims as "absent" objects and makes naïve or prejudiced generalisations concerning them. The development elicited two diametrically opposed reactions. At one level, hard core Orientalists mounted a spirited counter-attack. At another, there has been movement towards constructing what could be termed "post-Orientalist discourse."

As part of the counter-attack, Orientalist output adapted itself it to change and even witnessed a form of revival in response to the phenomena of "Islamic resurgence" in the 1970's and 1980's.[34] It continued to fend off its numerous critics, influence scholarship and even gain new adherents, including some "Orientalized Orientals" (non-Europeans who adopted the Orientalist outlook), most famous among whom are writers like V. S. Naipaul and Salman Rushdie.[35] The events of September 11 provided the diehard adherents of the discipline with a golden opportunity to launch a long-awaited come-back. The determined fight back to restore the credibility and prestige of Orientalism was spearheaded by figures such as Martin Kramer, former director of the Moshe Dayan Centre at Tel Aviv University, and his close associate, Daniel Pipes, director of the Philadelphia-based Middle East Forum, a right wing think tank. They were helped in this by such figures as Fouad Ajami of John Hopkins University, Robert Satloff of the Washington Institute, and Bernard Lewis, the reputed "doyen" of Orientalists who managed, at the age of 85, to produce a best-selling book immediately following the September 11 terror attacks.[36] The determined intellectual onslaught was accompanied by forms of public activism (including appeals to Congress, media campaigns and the formation in 2002 of a watch-dog named Campus Watch to name and shame "delinquent" academics). It was also whole-heartedly embraced by top officials in the Bush administration, putting the Middle Eastern Studies establishment on the defensive.

The core strategy of this group, which is militantly pro-Israel and has allied itself with American neo-conservatives and other right wing groups, was to blame and attempt to discredit the late Said. Kramer spearheaded the attack:

> For most academic commentators on things Islamic, 1978 is a watershed —not because a stern Shiite cleric inspired a revolution, but because a stern Columbia literature professor published a book. Edward Said's *Orientalism* persuaded them that their only legitimate role was to apologize and sympathize.[37]

Said's work, however, was preceded by earlier interventions, including some from within the "Orientalist" tradition itself (e.g. Marshall Hodgson), but mainly the input of an increasing number of scholars from within the Arab and Islamic traditions, including Anouar Abd el-Malek, A. L. Tibawi, Hisham Djait, Albert Hourani, Abdallah Laroui, Samir Amin, and Syed Hussein Alatas. Said's book, it has to be pointed out, signalled a "Eureka moment" in its own right, as its claims to unmask ethnocentric scholarly biases had a huge appeal to critical audiences in the period between the end of the Vietnam War (and the concurrent democratic revolutions in Greece, Spain, Portugal and Southern Africa) in the mid-1970's and the eruption of the Islamic Revolution in Iran and the Sandinista revolution in Nicaragua at the end of the decade.

The counterattack against Said started immediately after the publication of his book, which received scathing reviews from established Orientalists, including Bernard Lewis, Ernest Gellner and even Maxime Rodinson (who was lavishly praised in Said's book). However, the book weathered these critiques and the insistent subsequent tirades and established itself as a seminal text becoming, to the consternation of these numerous critics, "a nearly sacred doctrine in the American academy" (Teitelbaum and Litvak, 2006).

The new generation of determined campaigners described by Sadowski as "neo-Orientalists" (but who could equally be described as neo-conservatives), were not dispirited by this, especially since the September 11 attacks made it easy to link the otherwise largely theoretical debate to important current concerns. In his book *Ivory Towers on Sand: The Failure of Middle Eastern Studies in America* (2001), Kramer accused Middle Eastern scholars who do not subscribe to his unregenerate Orientalism of having failed to predict 9/11. Like Lewis' book (which was a collection of lectures delivered a couple of years earlier), Kramer's book had also been long in preparation and providentially released by the Washington Institute For Near East Policy just after the terrorist attacks in Manhattan and Washington. It thus made a powerful case by trying to link the alleged theoretical shortcomings of the discipline to its failure to be of use to American foreign policy makers. An energetic media campaign brought the book to the attention of academics and policy makers alike. When Campus Watch was launched by Kramer's associate Daniel Pipes a year later (in 2002), and Congress took steps to implement its recommendations shortly after that, academics had additional reasons to sit up and listen to this voice coming from beyond the tower walls.

But this counterattack would not have been complete without new attacks on the Prophet of Islam. Some of these works, like the absurdly controversial *Hagarism* (1977) by Patricia Crone and Michael Cook even predate Said's critique. This polemical book, which died a good death and received little serious attention from academia because of its far-fetched claims, tried not only to deny the historicity and mission of the Prophet, but to contest all Islamic history, using dubious sources. This did not deter more writers in this group from making a strenuous effort to peddle their wares, and a few works have appeared recently along the same lines of extreme bias. We need not bother the reader with details of these works, as some of them are already notorious because of their deliberate attempts to court controversy in order to boost the sales of otherwise uninteresting output. And as Rushdie's caricaturing of the Prophet has shown, they tend to have the opposite effect to what their authors intended: they motivate the public to seek genuine and credible sources of information about Islam and its Prophet.

On the other hand, the majority of western academics have moved in the other direction, trying to seek and promote a better understanding of Islamic culture, history and societies. The critique of Orientalism and its conscious and unconscious prejudices was only a first step. As part of it, a number of serious studies were conducted to examine specifically how the image of Muhammad has been projected in Western writings from medieval times to the present. We have already cited some of these works (such as those by Reeves and Bennett) and they are worthy of being consulted by those interested in a more detailed examination of how modern concepts of the Prophet and Islam has been shaped through the centuries. In this, they complement earlier works by Muslim scholars such as Qureshi, Jabal Muhammad Buaben and others.

These methodological critiques and historical accounts were accompanied and followed by new, better resourced and presented biographies of the Prophet Muhammad, either as separate works or as part of introductory works to Islam. These works have been produced by both Muslim and non-Muslim writers, including Karen Armstrong, Martin Lings, John Esposito and Gai Eton, to mention but a few. In this timely and important collection, we have chosen to cite only non-Muslim sources since these can be understood and related to by the wider audience we intend to reach through this short anthology. Our hope is that it would help promote a better understanding of the character and life of the Prophet Muhammad, as well as the religion of Islam, and by removing many prevalent misconceptions, help the cause of dialogue between cultures.

I

THE KORAN: COMMONLY CALLED THE ALKORAN OF MOHAMMED

BUT as Mohammed gave his Arabs the best religion he could, as well as the best laws, preferable, at least, to those of the ancient pagan law-givers, I confess I cannot see why he deserves not equal respect–though not with Moses or Jesus Christ, whose laws came really from Heaven, yet, with Minos or Numa, notwithstanding the distinction of a learned writer, who seems to think it a greater crime to make use of an imposture to set up a new religion, founded on the acknowledgment of one true God, and to destroy idolatry, than to use the same means to gain reception to rules and regulations for the more orderly practice of heathenism already established.

To be acquainted with the various laws and constitutions of civilized nations, especially of those who flourish in our own time, is, perhaps, the most useful part of knowledge...yet as the law of Mohammed, by reason of the odium it lies under, and the strangeness of the language in which it is written, has been so much neglected. I flatter myself some things in the following...I shall not regret the pains it has cost me...

I imagine it almost needless either to make an apology for publishing the following translation, or to go about to prove it a work of use as well as curiosity. They must have a mean opinion of the Christian religion, or be but ill grounded therein, who can apprehend any danger from so manifest a forgery: and if the religious and civil institutions of foreign nations are worth our knowledge, those of Mohammed, the lawgiver of the Arabians, and founder of an empire which in less than a century spread itself over a greater part of the world than the Romans were ever masters of, must needs be so; whether we consider their extensive obtaining, or our frequent intercourse with those who are governed thereby. I shall not here inquire into the reasons why the law of Mohammed has met with so unexampled a reception in the world (for they are greatly deceived who imagine it to have been propagated by the sword alone), or by what means it came to be embraced by nations which never felt the force of the Mohammedan arms, and even by those which stripped the Arabians of their conquests, and put an end to the sovereignty and very being of their Khalîfs: yet it seems as if there was something more than what is vulgarly imagined in a religion which has made so surprising a progress. But whatever use an impartial version of the Korân may be of in other respects, it is absolutely necessary to undeceive those who, from the ignorant or unfair translations which have appeared, have entertained too favourable an opinion of the original, and also to enable us effectually to expose the imposture; none of those who have hitherto undertaken that province, not excepting Dr. Prideaux himself, having succeeded to the satisfaction of the judicious, for want of being complete masters of the controversy. The writers of the Romish communion, in particular, are so far from having done any service in their refutations of Mohammedism, that by endeavouring to defend their idolatry and other superstitions, they have rather contributed to the increase of that aversion which the Mohammedans in general have to the Christian religion...

...I have not, in speaking of Mohammed or his Korân, allowed myself to use those opprobrious appellations, and unmannerly expressions, which seem to be the strongest arguments of several who have written against them. On the contrary, I have thought myself to treat both with common decency, and even to approve such particulars as seemed to me to deserve approbation: for how criminal soever Mohammed may have been in imposing a false religion on mankind, the praises due to his real virtues ought not to be denied him; nor can I do otherwise than applaud the candour of the pious and learned Spanhemius, who, though he owned him to have been a wicked impostor, yet acknowledged him to have been richly furnished with natural endowments, beautiful in his person, of a subtle wit, agreeable behaviour, showing liberality to the poor, courtesy to every one, fortitude against his enemies, and above all a high reverence for the name of GOD; severe against the perjured, adulterers, murderers, slanderers, prodigals, covetous, false witnesses, etc., a great preacher of patience, charity, mercy, beneficence, gratitude, honouring of parents and superiors, and a frequent celebrator of the divine praises.

Of the several translations of the Korân now extant, there is but one which tolerably represents the sense of the original; and that being in Latin, a new version became necessary, at least to an English reader. What Bibliander published for a Latin translation of that book deserves not the name of a translation; the unaccountable liberties therein taken and the numberless faults, both of omission and commission, leaving scarce any resemblance of the original. It was made near six hundred years ago, being finished in 1143, by Robertus Retenensis, an Englishman, with the assistance of Hermannus Dalmata, at the request of Peter, Abbot of Clugny, who paid them well for their pains.

From this Latin version was taken the Italian of Andrea Arrivabene, notwithstanding the pretences in his dedication of its being done immediately from the Arabic; wherefore it is no wonder if the transcript be yet more faulty and absurd than the copy.

About the end of the fifteenth century, Johannes Andreas, a native of Xativa in the kingdom of Valencia, who from a Mohammedan doctor became a Christian priest, translated not only the Korân, but also its glosses, and the seven books of the Sonna, out of Arabic into the Arragonian tongue, at the command of Martin Garcia, Bishop of Barcelona and Inquisitor of Arragon. Whether this translation were ever published or not I am wholly ignorant: but it may be presumed to have been the better done for being the work of one bred up in the

Mohammedan religion and learning; though his refutation of that religion, which has had several editions, gives no great idea of his abilities.

II

THE HERO AS PROPHET: MAHOMET

FROM the first rude times of Paganism among the Scandinavians in the North, we advance to a very different epoch of religion, among a very different people: Mahometanism among the Arabs. A great change; what a change and progress is indicated here, in the universal condition and thoughts of men!

The Hero is not now regarded as a God among his fellowmen; but as one God-inspired, as a Prophet. It is the second phase of Hero-worship: the first or oldest, we may say, has passed away without return; in the history of the world there will not again be any man, never so great, whom his fellowmen will take for a god...

We have chosen Mahomet not as the most eminent Prophet; but as the one we are freest to speak of. He is by no means the truest of Prophets; but I do esteem him a true one. Farther, as there is no danger of our becoming, any of us, Mahometans, I mean to say all the good of him I justly can. It is the way to get at his secret: let us try to understand what he meant with the world; what the world meant and means with him, will then be a more answerable question. Our current hypothesis about Mahomet, that he was a scheming Impostor, a False-hood incarnate, that his religion is a mere mass of quackery and fatuity, begins really to be now untenable to any one. The lies, which well-meaning zeal has heaped round this man, are disgraceful to ourselves only. When Pococke inquired of Grotius, Where the proof was of that story of the pigeon, trained to pick peas from Mahomet's ear, and pass for an angel dictating to him? Grotius answered that there was no proof! It is really time to dismiss all that. The word this man spoke has been the life-guidance now of a hundred and eighty millions of men these twelve hundred years. These hundred and eighty millions were made by God as well as we. A greater number of God's creatures believe in Mahomet's word at this hour, than in any other word whatever. Are we to suppose that it was a miserable piece of spiritual legerdemain, this which so many creatures of the Almighty have lived by and died by? I, for my part, cannot form any such supposition. I will believe most things sooner than that. One would be entirely at a loss what to think of this world at all, if quackery so grew and were sanctioned here.

Alas, such theories are very lamentable. If we would attain to knowledge of anything in God's true Creation, let us disbelieve them wholly! They are the product of an Age of Scepticism: they indicate the saddest spiritual paralysis, and mere death-life of the souls of men: more godless theory, I think, was never promulgated in this Earth. A false man found a religion? Why, a false man cannot build a brick house! If he do not know and follow truly the properties of mortar, burnt clay and what else be [sic] works in, it is no house that he makes, but a rubbish-heap. It will not stand for twelve centuries, to lodge a hundred and eighty millions; it will fall straightway. A man must conform himself to Nature's laws, be verily in communion with Nature and the truth of things, or Nature will answer him, No, not at all! Speciosities are specious – ah me! – a Cagliostro, many Cagliostros, prominent world-leaders, do prosper by their quackery, for a day. It is like a forged bank-note; they get it passed out of their worthless hands: others, not they, have to smart for it. Nature bursts up in fire-flames, French Revolutions and such like, proclaiming with terrible veracity that forged notes are forged.

The Hero as Prophet: Mahomet

But of a Great Man especially, of him I will venture to assert that it is incredible he should have been other than true. It seems to me the primary foundation of him, and of all that can lie in him, this. No Mirabeau, Napoleon, Burns, Cromwell, no man adequate to do anything, but is first of all in right earnest about it; what I call a sincere man. I should say sincerity, a deep, great, genuine sincerity, is the first characteristic of all men in any way heroic. Not the sincerity that calls itself sincere; ah no, that is a very poor matter indeed; − a shallow braggart conscious sincerity; oftenest self-conceit mainly. The Great Man's sincerity is of the kind he cannot speak of, is not conscious of: nay, I suppose, he is conscious rather of insincerity; for what man can walk accurately by the law of truth for one day? No, the Great Man does not boast himself sincere, far from that; perhaps does not ask himself if he is so: I would say rather, his sincerity does not depend on himself; he cannot help being sincere! The great Fact of Existence is great to him. Fly as he will, he cannot get out of the awful presence of this Reality. His mind is so made; he is great by that, first of all. Fearful and wonderful, real as Life, real as Death, is this Universe to him. Though all men should forget its truth, and walk in a vain show, he cannot. At all moments the Flame-image glares in upon him; undeniable, there, there! − I wish you to take this as my primary definition of a Great Man. A little man may have this, it is competent to all men that God has made: but a Great Man cannot be without it.

Such a man is what we call an original man; he comes to us at first-hand. A messenger he, sent from the Infinite Unknown with tidings to us. We may call him Poet, Prophet, God; − in one way or other, we all feel that the words he utters are as no other man's words. Direct from the Inner Fact of things; − he lives, and has to live, in daily communion with that. Hearsays cannot hide it from him; he is blind, homeless, miserable, following hearsays; it glares in upon him. Really his utterances, are they not a kind of "revelation;" − what we must call such for want of some other name? It is from the heart of the world that he comes; he is portion of the primal reality of things. God has made many revelations: but this man too, has not God made him, the latest and newest of all? The "inspiration of the Almighty giveth him understanding:" we must listen before all to him.

This Mahomet, then, we will in no wise consider as an Inanity and Theatricality, a poor conscious ambitious schemer; we cannot conceive him so. The rude message he delivered was a real one withal; an earnest confused voice from the unknown Deep. The man's words were not false, nor his workings here below; no Inanity and Simulacrum; a fiery mass of Life cast up from the great bosom of Nature herself. To kindle the world; the world's Maker had ordered it so. Neither can the faults, imperfections, insincerities even, of Mahomet, if such were never so well proved against him, shake this primary fact about him...

It was among this Arab people, so circumstanced, in the year 570 of our Era, that the man Mahomet was born. He was of the family of Hashem, of the Koreish tribe as we said; though poor, connected with the chief persons of his country. Almost at his birth he lost his Father; at the age of six years his Mother too, a woman noted for her beauty, her worth and sense: he fell to the charge of his Grandfather, an old man, a hundred years old. A good old man: Mahomet's Father, Abdallah, had been his youngest favorite son. He saw in Mahomet, with his old life-worn eyes, a century old, the lost Abdallah come back again, all that was left of Abdallah. He loved the little orphan Boy greatly; used to say, They must take care of that beautiful little Boy, nothing in their kindred was more precious than he. At his death, while the boy was still but two years old, he left him in charge to Abu Thaleb the eldest of the Uncles, as to him that now was head of the house. By this Uncle, a just and rational man as everything betokens, Mahomet was brought up in the best Arab way...

One other circumstance we must not forget: that he had no school-learning; of the thing we call school-learning none at all. The art of writing was but just introduced into Arabia; it seems to be the true opinion that Mahomet never could write! Life in the Desert, with its experiences, was all his education. What of this infinite Universe he, from his dim place, with his own eyes and thoughts, could take in, so much and no more of it was he to know. Curious, if we will reflect on it, this of having no books. Except by what he could see for himself, or hear of by uncertain rumor of speech in the obscure Arabian Desert, he could know nothing. The wisdom that had been before him or at a distance from him in the world, was in a manner as good as not there for him. Of the great brother souls, flame-beacons through so many lands and times, no one directly communicates with this great soul. He is alone there, deep down in the bosom of the Wilderness; has to grow up so, – alone with Nature and his own Thoughts.

But, from an early age, he had been remarked as a thoughtful man. His companions named him "Al Amin, The Faithful." A man of truth and fidelity; true in what he did, in what he spake and thought. They noted that he always meant something. A man rather taciturn in speech; silent when there was nothing to be said; but pertinent, wise, sincere, when he did speak; always throwing light on the matter. This is the only sort of speech worth speaking! Through life we find him to have been regarded as an altogether solid, brotherly, genuine man. A serious, sincere character; yet amiable, cordial, companionable, jocose even; – a good laugh in him withal: there are men whose laugh is as untrue as anything about them; who cannot laugh. One hears of Mahomet's beauty: his fine sagacious honest face, brown florid complexion, beaming black eyes; – I somehow like too that vein on the brow, which swelled up black when he was in anger: like the "horseshoe vein" in Scott's *Redgauntlet*. It was a kind of feature in the Hashem family, this black swelling vein in the brow; Mahomet had it prominent, as would appear. A spontaneous, passionate, yet just, true-meaning man! Full of wild faculty, fire and light; of wild worth, all uncultured; working out his life-task in the depths of the Desert there...

Ah no: this deep-hearted Son of the Wilderness, with his beaming black eyes and open social deep soul, had other thoughts in him than ambition. A silent great soul; he was one of those who cannot but be in earnest; whom Nature herself has appointed to be sincere. While others walk in formulas and hearsays, contented enough to dwell there, this man could not screen himself in formulas; he was alone with his own soul and the reality of things. The great Mystery of Existence, as I said, glared in upon him, with its terrors, with its splendors; no hearsays could hide that unspeakable fact, "Here am I!" Such sincerity, as we named it, has in very truth something of divine. The word of such a man is a Voice direct from Nature's own Heart. Men do and must listen to that as to nothing else; – all else is wind in comparison.

From of old, a thousand thoughts, in his pilgrimings and wanderings, had been in this man: What am I? What is this unfathomable Thing I live in, which men name Universe? What is Life; what is Death? What am I to believe? What am I to do? The grim rocks of Mount Hara, of Mount Sinai, the stern sandy solitudes answered not. The great Heaven rolling silent overhead, with its blue-glancing stars, answered not. There was no answer. The man's own soul, and what of God's inspiration dwelt there, had to answer!

It is the thing which all men have to ask themselves; which we too have to ask, and answer. This wild man felt it to be of infinite moment; all other things of no moment whatever in comparison. The jargon of argumentative Greek Sects, vague traditions of Jews, the stupid routine of Arab Idolatry: there was no answer in these. A Hero, as I repeat, has this first distinction, which indeed we may call first and last, the Alpha and Omega of his whole Heroism, That he looks through the shows of things into things. Use and wont, respectable hearsay, respectable formula: all these are good, or are not good. There is something behind and beyond all these, which all these must correspond with, be the image of, or they are − Idolatries; "bits of black wood pretending to be God;" to the earnest soul a mockery and abomination. Idolatries never so gilded, waited on by heads of the Koreish, will do nothing for this man. Though all men walk by them, what good is it? The great Reality stands glaring there upon him. He there has to answer it, or perish miserably. Now, even now, or else through all Eternity never! Answer it; thou must find an answer. − Ambition? What could all Arabia do for this man; with the crown of Greek Heraclius, of Persian Chosroes, and all crowns in the Earth; − what could they all do for him? It was not of the Earth he wanted to hear tell; it was of the Heaven above and of the Hell beneath. All crowns and sovereignties whatsoever, where would they in a few brief years be? To be Sheik of Mecca or Arabia, and have a bit of gilt wood put into your hand, − will that be one's salvation? I decidedly think, not. We will leave it altogether, this impostor hypothesis, as not credible; not very tolerable even, worthy chiefly of dismissal by us.

Mahomet had been wont to retire yearly, during the month Ramadhan, into solitude and silence; as indeed was the Arab custom;

a praiseworthy custom, which such a man, above all, would find natural and useful. Communing with his own heart, in the silence of the mountains; himself silent; open to the "small still voices:" it was a right natural custom! Mahomet was in his fortieth year, when having withdrawn to a cavern in Mount Hara, near Mecca, during this Ramadhan, to pass the month in prayer, and meditation on those great questions, he one day told his wife Kadijah, who with his household was with him or near him this year, That by the unspeakable special favor of Heaven he had now found it all out; was in doubt and darkness no longer, but saw it all. That all these Idols and Formulas were nothing, miserable bits of wood; that there was One God in and over all; and we must leave all Idols, and look to Him. That God is great; and that there is nothing else great! He is the Reality. Wooden Idols are not real; He is real. He made us at first, sustains us yet; we and all things are but the shadow of Him; a transitory garment veiling the Eternal Splendor. "Allah akbar, God is great;" – and then also "Islam," That we must submit to God. That our whole strength lies in resigned submission to Him, whatsoever He do to us. For this world, and for the other! The thing He sends to us, were it death and worse than death, shall be good, shall be best; we resign ourselves to God. – "If this be Islam," says Goethe, "do we not all live in Islam?" Yes, all of us that have any moral life; we all live so. It has ever been held the highest wisdom for a man not merely to submit to Necessity, – Necessity will make him submit, – but to know and believe well that the stern thing which Necessity had ordered was the wisest, the best, the thing wanted there. To cease his frantic pretension of scanning this great God's-World in his small fraction of a brain; to know that it had verily, though deep beyond his soundings, a Just Law, that the soul of it was Good; – that his part in it was to conform to the Law of the Whole, and in devout silence follow that; not questioning it, obeying it as unquestionable.

I say, this is yet the only true morality known. A man is right and invincible, virtuous and on the road towards sure conquest, precisely while he joins himself to the great deep Law of the World, in spite of all superficial laws, temporary appearances, profit-and-loss calculations; he is victorious while he co-operates with that great central Law, not victorious otherwise: – and surely his first chance of co-operating with it, or getting into the course of it, is to know with his whole soul that it is; that it is good, and alone good! This is the soul of Islam; it is properly the soul of Christianity; – for Islam is definable as a confused form of Christianity; had Christianity not been, neither had it been. Christianity also commands us, before all, to be resigned to God. We are to take no counsel with flesh and blood; give ear to no vain cavils, vain sorrows and wishes: to know that we know nothing; that the worst and cruelest to our eyes is not what it seems; that we have to receive whatsoever befalls us as sent from God above, and say, It is good and wise, God is great! "Though He slay me, yet will I trust in Him." Islam means in its way Denial of Self, Annihilation of Self. This is yet the highest Wisdom that Heaven has revealed to our Earth.

Such light had come, as it could, to illuminate the darkness of this wild Arab soul. A confused dazzling splendor as of life and Heaven, in the great darkness which threatened to be death: he called it revelation and the angel Gabriel; – who of us yet can know what to call it? It is the "inspiration of the Almighty" that giveth us understanding. To know; to get into the truth of anything, is ever a mystic act, – of which the best Logics can but babble on the surface. "Is not Belief the true god-announcing Miracle?" says Novalis. That Mahomet's whole soul, set in flame with this grand Truth vouchsafed him, should feel as if it were important and the only important thing, was very natural. That Providence had unspeakably honored him by revealing it, saving him from death and darkness; that he therefore was bound to make known the same to all creatures: this is what was meant by "Mahomet is the Prophet of God;" this too is not without its true meaning.

The good Kadijah, we can fancy, listened to him with wonder, with doubt: at length she answered: Yes, it was true this that he said. One can fancy too the boundless gratitude of Mahomet; and how of all the kindnesses she had done him, this of believing the earnest struggling word he now spoke was the greatest. "It is certain," says Novalis, "my Conviction gains infinitely, the moment another soul will believe in it." It is a boundless favor. He never forgot this good Kadijah. Long afterwards, 'Ayesha his young favorite wife, a woman who indeed distinguished herself among the Moslem, by all manner of qualities, through her whole long life; this young brilliant 'Ayesha was, one day, questioning him: "Now am not I better than Kadijah? She was a widow; old, and had lost her looks: you love me better than you did her?" – "No, by Allah!" answered Mahomet: "No, by Allah! She believed in me when none else would believe. In the whole world I had but one friend, and she was that!" – Seid, his Slave, also believed in him; these with his young Cousin Ali, Abu Thaleb's son, were his first converts.

He spoke of his Doctrine to this man and that; but the most treated it with ridicule, with indifference; in three years, I think, he had gained but thirteen followers. His progress was slow enough. His encouragement to go on, was altogether the usual encouragement that such a man in such a case meets...

Mahomet naturally gave offence to the Koreish, Keepers of the Caabah, superintendents of the Idols. One or two men of influence had joined him: the thing spread slowly, but it was spreading. Naturally he gave offence to everybody: Who is this that pretends to be wiser than we all; that rebukes us all, as mere fools and worshippers of wood! Abu Thaleb the good Uncle spoke with him: Could he not be silent about all that; believe it all for himself, and not trouble others, anger the chief men, endanger himself and them all, talking of it? Mahomet answered: If the Sun stood on his right hand and the Moon on his left, ordering him to hold his peace, he could not obey! No: there was something in this Truth he had got which was of Nature herself; equal in rank to Sun, or Moon, or whatsoever thing Nature had made. It would speak itself there, so long as the Almighty allowed it, in spite of Sun and Moon, and all Koreish and all men and things. It must do that, and could do no other. Mahomet answered so; and, they say, "burst into tears." Burst into tears: he felt that Abu Thaleb was good to him; that the task he had got was no soft, but a stern and great one...

In the thirteenth year of his mission, finding his enemies all banded against him, forty sworn men, one out of every tribe, waiting to take his life, and no continuance possible at Mecca for him any longer, Mahomet fled to the place then called Yathreb, where he had gained some adherents; the place they now call Medina, or "Medinat al Nabi, the City of the Prophet," from that circumstance. It lay some two hundred miles off, through rocks and deserts; not without great difficulty, in such mood as we may fancy, he escaped thither, and found welcome. The whole East dates its era from this Flight, hegira as they name it: the Year 1 of this Hegira is 622 of our Era, the fifty-third of Mahomet's Life... Hitherto Mahomet had professed to publish his Religion by the way of preaching and persuasion alone. But now, driven foully out of his native country, since unjust men had not only given no ear to his earnest Heaven's-message, the deep cry of his heart, but would not even let him live if he kept speaking it, – the wild Son of the Desert resolved to defend himself, like a man and Arab...

Much has been said of Mahomet's propagating his Religion by the sword. It is no doubt far nobler what we have to boast of the Christian Religion, that it propagated itself peaceably in the way of preaching and conviction. Yet withal, if we take this for an argument of the truth or falsehood of a religion, there is a radical mistake in it. The sword indeed: but where will you get your sword! Every new opinion, at its starting, is precisely in a minority of one. In one man's head alone, there it dwells as yet. One man alone of the whole world believes it; there is one man against all men. That he take a sword, and try to propagate with that, will do little for him. You must first get your sword! On the whole, a thing will propagate itself as it can. We do not find, of the Christian Religion either, that it always disdained the sword, when once it had got one. Charlemagne's conversion of the Saxons was not by preaching. I care little about the sword: I will allow a thing to struggle for itself in this world, with any sword or tongue or implement it has, or can lay hold of. We will let it preach, and pamphleteer, and fight, and to the uttermost bestir itself, and do, beak and claws, whatsoever is in it; very sure that it will, in the long-run, conquer nothing which does not deserve to be conquered. What is better than itself, it cannot put away, but only what is worse. In this great Duel, Nature herself is umpire, and can do no wrong: the thing which is deepest-rooted in Nature, what we call truest, that thing and not the other will be found growing at last.

Here however, in reference to much that there is in Mahomet and his success, we are to remember what an umpire Nature is; what a greatness, composure of depth and tolerance there is in her. You take wheat to cast into the Earth's bosom; your wheat may be mixed with chaff, chopped straw, barn-sweepings, dust and all imaginable rubbish; no matter: you cast it into the kind just Earth; she grows the wheat, – the whole rubbish she silently absorbs, shrouds it in, says nothing of the rubbish... So everywhere in Nature! She is true and not a lie; and yet so great, and just, and motherly in her truth. She requires of a thing only that it be genuine of heart; she will protect it if so; will not, if not so... The genuine essence of Truth never dies...

Out of all that rubbish of Arab idolatries, argumentative theologies, traditions, subtleties, rumors and hypotheses of Greeks and Jews, with their idle wire-drawings, this wild man of the Desert, with his wild sincere heart, earnest as death and life, with his great flashing natural eyesight, had seen into the kernel of the matter. Idolatry is nothing: these Wooden Idols of yours, "ye rub them with oil and wax, and the flies stick on them," – these are wood, I tell you! They can do nothing for you; they are an impotent blasphemous presence; a horror and abomination, if ye knew them. God alone is; God alone has power; He made us, He can kill us and keep us alive: "Allah akbar, God is great." Understand that His will is the best for you; that howsoever sore to flesh and blood, you will find it the wisest, best: you are bound to take it so; in this world and in the next, you have no other thing that you can do...

Sincerity, in all senses, seems to me the merit of the Koran; what had rendered it precious to the wild Arab men. It is, after all, the first and last merit in a book; gives rise to merits of all kinds, – nay, at bottom, it alone can give rise to merit of any kind. Curiously, through these incondite masses of tradition, vituperation, complaint, ejaculation in the Koran, a vein of true direct insight, of what we might almost call poetry, is found straggling. The body of the Book is made up of mere tradition, and as it were vehement enthusiastic extempore preaching. He returns forever to the old stories of the Prophets as they went current in the Arab memory: how Prophet after Prophet, the Prophet Abraham, the Prophet Hud, the Prophet Moses, Christian and other real and fabulous Prophets, had come to this Tribe and to that, warning men of their sin; and been received by them even as he, Mahomet was, – which is a great solace to him. These things he repeats ten, perhaps twenty times; again and ever again, with wearisome iteration; has never done repeating them… But curiously, through all this, comes ever and anon some glance as of the real thinker and seer. He has actually an eye for the world, this Mahomet: with a certain directness and rugged vigor, he brings home still, to our heart, the thing his own heart has been opened to. I make but little of his praises of Allah, which many praise; they are borrowed I suppose mainly from the Hebrew, at least they are far surpassed there. But the eye that flashes direct into the heart of things, and sees the truth of them; this is to me a highly interesting object. Great Nature's own gift; which she bestows on all; but which only one in the thousand does not cast sorrowfully away: it is what I call sincerity of vision; the test of a sincere heart.

Mahomet can work no miracles; he often answers impatiently: I can work no miracles. I? "I am a Public Preacher;" appointed to preach this doctrine to all creatures. Yet the world, as we can see, had really from of old been all one great miracle to him. Look over the world, says he; is it not wonderful, the work of Allah; wholly "a sign to you," if your eyes were open! This Earth, God made it for you; "appointed paths in it;" you can live in it, go to and fro on it. The clouds in the dry country of Arabia, to Mahomet they are very wonderful: Great clouds, he says, born in the deep bosom of the Upper Immensity, where do they come from! They hang there, the great black monsters; pour down their rain-deluges "to revive a dead earth," and grass springs, and "tall leafy palm-trees with their date-clusters hanging round. Is not that a sign?" Your cattle too, – Allah made them; serviceable dumb creatures; they change the grass into milk; you have your clothing from them, very strange creatures; they come ranking home at evening-time, "and," adds he, "and are a credit to you!" Ships also, – he talks often about ships: Huge moving mountains, they spread out their cloth wings, go bounding through the water there, Heaven's wind driving them; anon they lie motionless, God has withdrawn the wind, they lie dead, and cannot stir! Miracles? cries he: What miracle would you have? Are not you yourselves there? God made you, "shaped you out of a little clay." Ye were small once; a few years ago ye were not at all. Ye have beauty, strength, thoughts, "ye have compassion on one another." Old age comes on you, and gray hairs;

your strength fades into feebleness; ye sink down, and again are not. "Ye have compassion on one another:" this struck me much: Allah might have made you having no compassion on one another, – how had it been then! This is a great direct thought, a glance at first-hand into the very fact of things. Rude vestiges of poetic genius, of whatsoever is best and truest, are visible in this man. A strong untutored intellect; eyesight, heart: a strong wild man, – might have shaped himself into Poet, King, Priest, any kind of Hero.

To his eyes it is forever clear that this world wholly is miraculous. He sees what, as we said once before, all great thinkers, the rude Scandinavians themselves, in one way or other, have contrived to see: That this so solid-looking material world is, at bottom, in very deed, Nothing; is a visual and factual Manifestation of God's power and presence, – a shadow hung out by Him on the bosom of the void Infinite; nothing more. The mountains, he says, these great rock-mountains, they shall dissipate themselves "like clouds;" melt into the Blue as clouds do, and not be! He figures the Earth, in the Arab fashion, Sale tells us, as an immense Plain or flat Plate of ground, the mountains are set on that to steady it. At the Last Day they shall disappear "like clouds;" the whole Earth shall go spinning, whirl itself off into wreck, and as dust and vapor vanish in the Inane. Allah withdraws his hand from it, and it ceases to be. The universal empire of Allah, presence everywhere of an unspeakable Power, a Splendor, and a Terror not to be named, as the true force, essence and reality, in all things whatsoever, was continually clear to this man. What a modern talks of by the name, Forces of Nature, Laws of Nature; and does not figure as a divine thing; not even as one thing at all, but as a set of things, undivine enough, – salable, curious, good for propelling steamships! With our Sciences and Cyclopaedias, we are apt to forget the divineness, in those laboratories of ours. We ought not to forget it! That once well forgotten, I know not what else were worth remembering. Most sciences, I think were then a very dead thing; withered, contentious, empty; – a thistle in late autumn. The best science, without this, is but as the dead timber; it is not the growing tree and forest, – which gives ever-new timber, among other things! Man cannot know either, unless he can worship in some way. His knowledge is a pedantry, and dead thistle, otherwise.

Much has been said and written about the sensuality of Mahomet's Religion; more than was just. The indulgences, criminal to us, which he permitted, were not of his appointment; he found them practiced, unquestioned from immemorial time in Arabia; what he did was to curtail them, restrict them, not on one but on many sides. His Religion is not an easy one: with rigorous fasts, lavations, strict complex formulas, prayers five times a day, and abstinence from wine, it did not "succeed by being an easy religion." As if indeed any religion, or cause holding of religion, could succeed by that! It is a calumny on men to say that they are roused to heroic action by ease, hope of pleasure, recompense, – sugar-plums of any kind, in this world or the next! ... It is not to taste sweet things, but to do noble and true things, and vindicate himself under God's Heaven as a god-made Man, that the poorest son of Adam dimly longs... Not by flattering our appetites; no, by awakening the Heroic that slumbers in every heart, can any Religion gain followers.

Mahomet himself, after all that can be said about him, was not a sensual man. We shall err widely if we consider this man as a common voluptuary, intent mainly on base enjoyments, – nay on enjoyments of any kind. His household was of the frugalest; his common diet barley-bread and water: sometimes for months there was not a fire once lighted on his hearth. They record with just pride that he would mend his own shoes, patch his own cloak. A poor, hard-toiling, ill-provided man; careless of what vulgar men toil for. Not a bad man, I should say; something better in him than hunger of any sort, – or these wild Arab men, fighting and jostling three-and-twenty years at his hand, in close contact with him always, would not have reverenced him so! They were wild men, bursting ever and anon into quarrel, into all kinds of fierce sincerity; without right worth and manhood, no man could have commanded them. They called him Prophet, you say? Why, he stood there face to face with them; bare, not enshrined in any mystery; visibly clouting his own cloak, cobbling his own shoes; fighting, counselling, ordering in the midst of them: they must have seen what kind of a man he was, let him be called what you like! No emperor with his tiaras was obeyed as this man in a cloak of his own clouting. During three-and-twenty years of rough actual trial. I find something of a veritable Hero necessary for that, of itself.

The Hero as Prophet: Mahomet

His last words are a prayer; broken ejaculations of a heart struggling up, in trembling hope, towards its Maker. We cannot say that his religion made him worse; it made him better; good, not bad. Generous things are recorded of him: when he lost his Daughter, the thing he answers is, in his own dialect, every way sincere, and yet equivalent to that of Christians, "The Lord giveth, and the Lord taketh away; blessed be the name of the Lord." He answered in like manner of Seid, his emancipated well-beloved Slave, the second of the believers. Seid had fallen in the War of Tabuc, the first of Mahomet's fightings with the Greeks. Mahomet said, It was well; Seid had done his Master's work, Seid had now gone to his Master: it was all well with Seid. Yet Seid's daughter found him weeping over the body; – the old gray-haired man melting in tears! "What do I see?" said she. – "You see a friend weeping over his friend." – He went out for the last time into the mosque, two days before his death; asked, If he had injured any man? Let his own back bear the stripes. If he owed any man? A voice answered, "Yes, me three drachms," borrowed on such an occasion. Mahomet ordered them to be paid: "Better be in shame now," said he, "than at the Day of Judgment." – You remember Kadijah, and the "No, by Allah!" Traits of that kind show us the genuine man, the brother of us all, brought visible through twelve centuries, – the veritable Son of our common Mother.

Withal I like Mahomet for his total freedom from cant. He is a rough self-helping son of the wilderness; does not pretend to be what he is not. There is no ostentatious pride in him; but neither does he go much upon humility: he is there as he can be, in cloak and shoes of his own clouting; speaks plainly to all manner of Persian Kings, Greek Emperors, what it is they are bound to do; knows well enough, about himself, "the respect due unto thee." In a life-and-death war with Bedouins, cruel things could not fail; but neither are acts of mercy, of noble natural pity and generosity wanting. Mahomet makes no apology for the one, no boast of the other. They were each the free dictate of his heart; each called for, there and then. Not a mealy-mouthed man! A candid ferocity, if the case call for it, is in him; he does not mince matters! The War of Tabuc is a thing he often speaks of: his men refused, many of them, to march on that occasion; pleaded the heat of the weather, the harvest, and so forth; he can never forget that. Your harvest? It lasts for a day. What will become of your harvest through all Eternity? Hot weather? Yes, it was hot; "but Hell will be hotter!" Sometimes a rough sarcasm turns up: He says to the unbelievers, Ye shall have the just measure of your deeds at that Great Day. They will be weighed out to you; ye shall not have short weight! – Everywhere he fixes the matter in his eye; he sees it: his heart, now and then, is as if struck dumb by the greatness of it. "Assuredly," he says: that word, in the Koran, is written down sometimes as a sentence by itself: "Assuredly."

No Dilettantism in this Mahomet; it is a business of Reprobation and Salvation with him, of Time and Eternity: he is in deadly earnest about it! Dilettantism, hypothesis, speculation, a kind of amateur-search for Truth, toying and coquetting with Truth: this is the sorest sin. The root of all other imaginable sins. It consists in the heart and soul of the man never having been open to Truth; – "living in a vain show." Such a man not only utters and produces falsehoods, but is himself a falsehood. The rational moral principle, spark of the Divinity, is sunk deep in him, in quiet paralysis of life-death. The very falsehoods of Mahomet are truer than the truths of such a man. He is the insincere man: smooth-polished, respectable in some times and places; inoffensive, says nothing harsh to anybody; most cleanly, – just as carbonic acid is, which is death and poison.

We will not praise Mahomet's moral precepts as always of the superfinest sort; yet it can be said that there is always a tendency to good in them; that they are the true dictates of a heart aiming towards what is just and true. The sublime forgiveness of Christianity, turning of the other cheek when the one has been smitten, is not here: you are to revenge yourself, but it is to be in measure, not overmuch, or beyond justice. On the other hand, Islam, like any great Faith, and insight into the essence of man, is a perfect equalizer of men: the soul of one believer outweighs all earthly kingships; all men, according to Islam too, are equal. Mahomet insists not on the propriety of giving alms, but on the necessity of it: he marks down by law how much you are to give, and it is at your peril if you neglect. The tenth part of a man's annual income, whatever that may be, is the property of the poor, of those that are afflicted and need help. Good all this: the natural voice of humanity, of pity and equity dwelling in the heart of this wild Son of Nature speaks *so*...

In the Koran there is really very little said about the joys of Paradise; they are intimated rather than insisted on. Nor is it forgotten that the highest joys even there shall be spiritual; the pure Presence of the Highest, this shall infinitely transcend all other joys. He says, "Your salutation shall be, Peace." Salam, Have Peace! – the thing that all rational souls long for, and seek, vainly here below, as the one blessing. "Ye shall sit on seats, facing one another: all grudges shall be taken away out of your hearts." All grudges! Ye shall love one another freely; for each of you, in the eyes of his brothers, there will be Heaven enough...

On the whole, we will repeat that this Religion of Mahomet's is a kind of Christianity; has a genuine element of what is spiritually highest looking through it, not to be hidden by all its imperfections. The Scandinavian God Wish, the god of all rude men, – this has been enlarged into a Heaven by Mahomet; but a Heaven symbolical of sacred Duty, and to be earned by faith and well-doing, by valiant action, and a divine patience which is still more valiant. It is Scandinavian Paganism, and a truly celestial element superadded to that. Call it not false; look not at the falsehood of it, look at the truth of it. For these twelve centuries, it has been the religion and life-guidance of the fifth part of the whole kindred of Mankind. Above all things, it has been a religion heartily believed. These Arabs believe their religion, and try to live by it! No Christians, since the early ages, or only perhaps the English Puritans in modern times, have ever stood by their Faith as the Moslem do by theirs, – believing it wholly, fronting Time with it, and Eternity with it. This night the watchman on the streets of Cairo when he cries, "Who goes?" will hear from the passenger, along with his answer, "There is no God but God." Allah akbar, Islam, sounds through the souls, and whole daily existence, of these dusky millions. Zealous missionaries preach it abroad among Malays, black Papuans, brutal Idolaters; – displacing what is worse, nothing that is better or good.

To the Arab Nation it was as a birth from darkness into light; Arabia first became alive by means of it. A poor shepherd people, roaming unnoticed in its deserts since the creation of the world: a Hero-Prophet was sent down to them with a word they could believe: see, the unnoticed becomes world-notable, the small has grown world-great; within one century afterwards, Arabia is at Grenada on this hand, at Delhi on that; – glancing in valor and splendor and the light of genius, Arabia shines through long ages over a great section of the world. Belief is great, life-giving. The history of a Nation becomes fruitful, soul-elevating, great, so soon as it believes. These Arabs, the man Mahomet, and that one century, – is it not as if a spark had fallen, one spark, on a world of what seemed black unnoticeable sand; but lo, the sand proves explosive powder, blazes heaven-high from Delhi to Grenada! I said, the Great Man was always as lightning out of Heaven; the rest of men waited for him like fuel, and then they too would flame.

III

HISTOIRE DE LA TURQUIE

NEVER has a man set himself, voluntarily or involuntarily, a more sublime aim, since this aim was superhuman: to subvert superstitions which had been interposed between man and his Creator, to render God unto man and man unto God; to restore the rational and sacred idea of divinity amidst the chaos of the material and disfigured gods of idolatry, then existing.

Never has a mane undertaken a work so far beyond human power with so feeble means, for he had in the conception as well as in the execution of such a great design no other instrument than himself, and no other aid, except a handful of men living in a corner of the desert. Finally, never has a man accomplished such a huge and lasting revolution in the world...

If greatness of purpose, smallness of means, and astounding results are the three criteria of human genius, who could dare to compare any great man in modem history with Muhammad? The most famous men created arms, laws and empires only. They founded, if anything at all, no more than material powers which often crumbled away before their eyes. This man moved not only armies, legislation, empires, peoples and dynasties, but millions of men in one-third of the then-inhabited world; and more than that he moved the altars, the gods, the religions, the ideas, the beliefs and souls... On the basis of a Book, every letter of which has become law, he created a spiritual nationality, which blended together peoples of every tongue and of every race. He has left us – as the indelible characteristic of this Muslim nationality – the hatred of false gods and the passion for the One and Immaterial God... The conquest of one-third of the earth to his dogma was his miracle; rather it was not the miracle of a man but that of reason.

His life, his meditations, his heroic revilings against the superstitions of his country, and his boldness in defying the furies of idolatry, his firmness in enduring them for thirteen years at Makkah, his acceptance of the role of public scorn and almost of being a victim of his fellow countrymen: all these and finally, his migration, his incessant preaching, his wars against odds, his faith in his success and his superhuman security in misfortune, his forbearance in victory, his ambition, which was entirely devoted to one idea and in no manner striving for an empire, his endless prayers, his mystic conversations with God, his death and his triumph after death – all these... (served) to affirm conviction which gave him power to restore a creed. This creed was twofold: the unity of God and the immateriality of God; the former telling what God is, the latter telling what God is not; the one overthrowing false gods with the sword, the other starting an idea with the words.

Philosopher, orator, apostle, legislator, warrior, conqueror of ideas, restorer of rational dogmas, of a cult without images; the founder of twenty terrestrial empires and of one spiritual empire, that is Muhammad. As regards all standards by which human greatness may be measured, we may well ask, is there any man greater than he?

IV

MOHAMMED: THE MAN AND HIS FAITH

A new form of religious life like that of Islam is not merely a body of doctrine or a system of ritual. It is, when profoundly regarded, a form of spiritual energy, a living seed. It develops its own life and attracts other spiritual life to itself, according to a law whose significance and purpose is completely revealed only after an extended development. There is originality enough in Mohammed's achievement in catching up into a vital and adaptable personal synthesis the spiritual potentialities of his age. Truly 'My prayers and my worship and my life and my death are unto God, Lord of the Worlds. He hath no associate. This am I commanded, and I am the first of the Muslims' (Sura 6, 163). The first of the Muslims! Mohammed is absolutely justified in so designating himself He is the first representative of a new and independent religious type. Even to-day, after a period of development of thirteen centuries, one may clearly discern in genuine Islamic piety the uniqueness which is ultimately derived from its founder's personal experience of God.

Hitherto the nature of Mohammedan piety has generally been

rather unjustly ignored by Western students of religion. If one were to seek out the cause for this, it would not suffice to refer to ignorance, or to the reaction of old dogmatic prejudices against the 'false prophet,' or to political hatred of 'the dog of a Turk.' The cause lies deeper, and may perhaps be best expressed by the proverb: Relatives understand each other least of all. A Christian sees much in Islam which reminds him of his own religion, but he sees it in an extremely distorted form. He finds ideas and statements of belief clearly related to those of his own religion, but which, nevertheless, turn off into strangely different paths. Islam is so familiar to us that we pass it by with the careless indifference with which we ignore that which we know and know only too well. And yet it is not familiar enough to us to enable us really to understand its uniqueness, and the spirit by which Islam has won its own place in the sphere of religion, a place which it still rightly occupies by virtue of its very existence. We found it much easier to understand religions that are completely new and strange to us – as, for example, the religions of India and China. A greater degree of insight and of spiritual freedom is required of him who would understand the Arabian Prophet and his book…

The concepts of the period of Enlightenment permitted a more just estimate of Mohammed's personality. In their naïve fashion the thinkers of this period often evaluated the outstanding wisdom and virtue of ancient lawgivers and founders of religions, and stressed the reasonableness of alien faiths, praising them at the expense of Christianity. They extended to Islam this benevolent evaluation of the non-Christian religions. Sale, who in 1734 published a translation of the Koran which for long remained the standard version, compared Mohammed with Numa and Theseus. A few years previously De Boulainvilliers had written a Life of Mohammed with the avowed purpose of demonstrating the superiority of Islam to Christianity. He portrayed Mohammed as a wise and enlightened lawgiver, who sought to establish a reasonable religion in place of the dubious dogmas of Judaism and Christianity. The same attitude is expressed in Savary's translation of the Koran, which was published in 1752. He regards Mohammed as one of those unusual personalities occasionally appearing in history, who remake their environment and enlist men in their triumphant train. Savary thinks that anyone studying Mohammed's career must marvel at the achievements of which human genius is capable when circumstances are favourable. Although born as an idolater, Mohammed rose to the worship of one God. In the course of his travels he observed how the divided Christians poured condemnation upon one another, and how the Jews, 'the scum of the nations,' obstinately clung to their laws. In contrast with this Mohammed sought to establish a new universal religion, by setting up a simple dogma which contained only what the reason must accept, namely, belief in one God who rewards virtue and punishes transgressors.

Savary was an enlightened Westerner, who, to be sure, justly refused to call Mohammed a prophet, but who was nevertheless forced to recognize him as one of the greatest men who ever lived... On Friday, March 8, 1840, when Carlyle began his description of Mohammed's personality in his second lecture on "Heroes and Hero Worship," he stated that the prevalent view was that Mohammed was an impostor, an incarnation of falsehood, and that his religion was a combination of charlatanism and stupidity. But in Carlyle's opinion such a view is a reflection upon ourselves. One hundred and eighty million human beings confess Islam as the true religion. For countless people Mohammed's words have been the guiding star of their lives. Can it be possible that so many creatures, created by God, have lived and died for something which must be regarded as a tragic fraud? What are we to think of this world, if charlatanism really has such power over the minds of men? This hypothesis is a sad creation of the age of scepticism, and is more indicative of mental paralysis and spiritual death. A more godless theory has never been propounded.

In Carlyle's opinion Mohammed was sincere, as every great man is sincere, because he had to be. He was genuinely sincere in spite of his deep consciousness of a lack of sincerity. The great fact of existence overwhelmed him; he could not escape its grip. Others might ignore this fact, and live in empty vanity, but to him the reality of life seemed terribly wonderful, and a flaming vision before his eyes. Such a man is a great man. We may also call him an original man, a messenger who brings us news of the infinite and the unknown. We might call him a poet or a prophet, for we feel that the words which he speaks are not the words of an ordinary man. They have their immediate source in the inner reality of things, since he lives in constant fellowship with this reality. For Carlyle's romantic idealism the man of genius is at once the highest revelation and the symbol of that Divine power which is the innermost reality of existence. Mohammed had seen the light of the Divine law of existence, 'a confused dazzling splendour of life and heaven, in the great darkness which threatened to be death: he called it revelation and the angel Gabriel – who of us yet can know what to call it?'

Mohammed's religious integrity rests, then, upon the fact that he himself was one of those great personalities who are expressions of the creative life of God, and who have, therefore, an intuitive contact with this creative life, a spontaneous revelation of God. The sacred book and the angel are only symbolical expressions of this experience of God, expressions which Carlyle evidently regards as rather unessential. In this respect the romantic philosophy of intuition adopts approximately the same point of view as that of the Enlightenment.

For us also the originality, the immediacy, and the freshness of religious experience may be proof of the genuineness of inspiration. Unfortunately, however, it depends very much upon the attitude of the observer, and his ability to enter sympathetically into the object, whether he will acknowledge the presence of this criterion. There are students of religion, even those who are not bound by doctrinal scruples, who cannot, in Carlyle's sense, discover anything genuine and immediate in Mohammed, even though they have the best of intentions. ...That Mohammed's inspiration was genuine in the psychological sense has already been emphasized incidentally. It is hardly believable that a man could have won such absolute confidence, or could have made such an impression upon his surroundings, had he not possessed an overwhelming and convincing faith in his own message. Mohammed regarded his call with the utmost sincerity; he felt his heart tremble before the King of the Judgment Day, and he responded to His prophetic commission with fear and trembling. 'But if Mohammed had fabricated concerning us any sayings, we had surely seized him by the right hand, and had cut through the vein of his neck. Nor would we have withheld any of you from him' (69, 44–47). Allah stations watchmen who walk before and behind His Apostle to make sure that he is faithfully transmitting His message. One need not be especially well disposed to the personal quality of a religious proclamation in order to hear the footsteps of these stern watchmen in the fearful warnings of the Prophet, as well as in the drastic expressions of his sorrow and perplexity when no one heeds his preaching.

Many inspired men have succeeded in performing signs and wonders which have confirmed their claim of a call. The legends of the miracles of holy men are not always fables created in a vacuum; they may often describe actual experiences, although these have undergone a peculiar reconstruction. Of course, such miracles are often produced in all subjective honesty, but we can readily understand how deception might be employed, either consciously or unconsciously. Mohammed rejected every request to pose as a wonder-worker, and emphatically denied all superstitions in regard to his own person. He is only a man like other men; he has no recourse to heavenly resources; he is not even the master of his own fate, to say nothing of the fate of others. To be sure, these statements originated in Mecca. But there is nothing to show that Mohammed attempted to exploit the superstitious reverence for his person which the believers in Medina are supposed to have shown him…

At all events, in important matters he did not attempt to advance his authority or safeguard his position by means of alleged miracles. I know of only two exceptions. The one occurred at Bedr, where he threw a handful of sand at the enemy in the belief that this magic act would help to gain the victory. And it seems quite understandable that in this moment of highest tension, when his cause really hung in the balance, he should receive a sign of such significance from Allah. In fact, it is just as natural as it was for Isaiah, who ordinarily never posed as a wonder-worker, to have no scruples about promising every sign which King Ahaz desired in order to win him over to his daring faith. The other exception is Mohammed's midnight journey to Jerusalem. This was a dream to which he seems to refer in such a way as to prove that he attributed to it the same validity that he attributed to other experiences.

Islamic dogma has depicted the Prophet as sinless. He never committed a deliberate sin, and at the most he may have been guilty only of some involuntary unintentional act which might be reckoned among the lighter sins. It is a likeable characteristic of Mohammed that he never claimed perfection or infallibility, but always admitted frankly that he was guilty of shortcomings and mistakes like other men. According to Sura 48, 1, the 'undoubted victory,' that is, the conquest of Mecca, is a sign that Allah has forgiven the Prophet his earlier and later sins. The touching story of the pearl necklace, which Mohammed gave to 'Ayesha, and which caused him a sleepless night, shows that, in spite of his lofty opinion of his position as the Apostle of Allah, he still retained something of that simplicity of heart characteristic of the upright man. Not once in his career did he feel invulnerable to errors and mistakes. That he was not disloyal to his holy task seems to him only an act of the special grace of God (17, 75–77). Like other prophets Mohammed prayed: 'O our Lord! forgive us our sins and our mistakes in this our work; and set our feet firm; and help us against the unbelieving people' (3, 141). On the whole it may be said that Mohammed exhibited as much humility and self-criticism as one could reasonably expect from an Apostle of Allah whose work was crowned with such striking outward success. That he so resolutely withstood the temptations to pride and self-exaltation involved in his position shows that he was a man of moral sincerity.

In the problem of Mohammed's personal integrity is also involved the question of the extent to which he himself lived up to the religious and moral ideal which he created. He did not hesitate to set himself up as a model for believers; 'A noble pattern had ye in God's Apostle, for all who hope in God and in the latter days' (33, 21), just as St. Paul expressed the wish that his converts might become like him in all things except his chains. Such moral self-consciousness doubtless presupposes an absence of apparent contradiction between Mohammed's religious ideal of life and his personal conduct. His religious morality was on the whole of an ascetic nature. To be sure, the things of the world are not in themselves evil, but they easily become a snare and cause one to forget the world to come. Did Mohammed succeed in guarding himself from the temptations of the world, or did he fall a victim in Medina, as is frequently claimed, to temptations of power, honour, and enjoyment?

The oldest collections of tradition often depict the Prophet as an emaciated penitent. According to one writer, the habit of eating until one is satisfied was a new fad, unknown to the pious men of the first generation. The Prophet said: 'Adam's son filled no vessel which is more evil than his stomach' – and he acted accordingly. 'Ayesha relates that he never ate to satiety, and that he never asked for or desired food when he was with his wives. He ate and drank only what was given to him. The members of Mohammed's family lived in such poverty that they really suffered privation. Anas Ibn Malik, Mohammed's valet, tells that when Fatima once came to her father with bread, he said: 'This is the first bite which your father has tasted in three days.' Abu Huraira, the authority for a great number of traditions which sound a strictly ascetic-pietistic note, relates that the Prophet became so hungry that he tightly bound his stomach and his loins in order to relieve his suffering. The same writer states that month after month passed in Mohammed's family without a fire being kindled in the house to bake bread or pastry. 'Upon what do you live?' the questioner asked, and Abu Huraira answered: 'Upon the two black things: dates and water.' – 'Ayesha tells how she once received a leg of lamb from her father, and how she and Allah's Apostle attempted to devour it in the dark – 'In the dark?' asked the listeners; 'had you no lamps?' – 'If we had had lamps we would have used up our oil long ago,'' 'Ayesha replied. – On another occasion she suddenly burst into tears, and when those present asked why she wept, she answered: 'I have heard that you are now in the habit of eating yourself so full that you need medicine in order to heal your stomachs. Then I thought of your Prophet. As long as he lived he never filled his stomach with two kinds of food. When he ate his fill of dates, then he ate no bread. When he satisfied his hunger with bread, then he ate no dates. When the Prophet died he had put his coat of mail in pawn with a Jew for three measures of meal. Another tradition tells of his simplicity and his freedom from pretension.' When Allah sent Mohammed He said: "This is My Prophet, My elect, accept him as a friend and obey his rules and ways. No portals prevent access to him and no guard stands in the way. No large keys are brought to him in the morning and at night. He clothes himself in rough garments, rides upon a donkey, and licks his fingers after he has eaten." He says: "Whoever is not willing to follow my Sunna does not belong to me."

...It is told that some of the companions of the Prophet boasted of their pious works in his presence. One man said: 'I am unmarried,' another: 'I eat no meat,' a third: 'I sleep on the bare ground,' and a fourth: 'I fast continually.' Then Mohammed said: 'Praise be to Allah! I fast and I eat, I keep vigil and I sleep, and I am married. And whoever is not willing to follow my Sunna does not belong to me.' The attempt is made to show that the Prophet lived like an ordinary man. There was nothing of bigotry or of the hyper-spiritual in his nature. Several pious men came to Zaid Ibn Thabit and said: 'Tell us about the characteristics of the Prophet.' He answered: 'I was his neighbour, and when the revelation came to him I wrote it down for him. When we conversed about this world he also spoke of it, and when we conversed about food, he also spoke of that. Do you desire that I should tell you all about that?'

In these contrasting statements we actually have, then, not so much descriptions of the circumstances of the domestic life of Mohammed as formal principles relating to ethical questions, along with the attempt to illuminate and support these principles by appealing to the authority of the Prophet's exemplary life. In Islam there were pious men of strict habits, pietists and ascetics, who wished to follow the narrow road of abstinence, and they fought against every form of worldly mindedness and fleshly desire. Others were of the opinion that one ought to be temperate in one's piety and participate in some of the joys of life. Hence what the traditions tell us about Mohammed's private life is comparatively worthless as a historical source...

There is every indication, however, that even in Medina Mohammed lived on the whole in rather modest circumstances, and adhered to the moderately ascetic ideal which he defends in the Koran. We are there told that he defended himself against all possible accusations of the Jews or 'hypocrites,' and of the doubters among the population of Medina. But there is no mention of complaints concerning luxury, splendour, or high living. Therefore we are right in assuming that the life of the Prophet presented no occasion for criticism on this point...

The genuineness and sincerity of Mohammed's piety, and the honesty of his belief in his religious call, are indisputable... According to the tradition of Islam, the Prophet's personality was characterized by unique kindliness, amiability, and friendliness. He was never the first to withdraw his hand when he greeted anyone, and he was never the first to turn his face away when conversing with another. No one, whether a red man or a black (that is, an Arab or a negro) ever spoke to him without receiving a reply, and he often picked up discarded dates and put them into his mouth because he thought that they might be a gift and did not wish to offend the giver. He greeted everyone, slaves and little children as well. When 'Ayesha was questioned as to the conduct of the Prophet in private life, she replied: 'The most gentle and noble of men. Otherwise he was like other men, except that he loved to laugh and smile.' It is surely no accident that our sources so often refer to this irresistible smile. It is evident that Mohammed had a remarkable gift for winning people. Often, as with a magic stroke, he succeeded in transforming dissatisfaction into surrender and dislike into attraction. He showed special kindness to his former enemies.

V

MUHAMMAD: PROPHET AND STATESMAN

MUHAMMAD, according to some apparently authentic accounts, was of average height or a little above the average. His chest and shoulders were broad, and altogether he was of sturdy build. His arms were long, and his hands and feet rough. His forehead was large and prominent, and he had a hooked nose and large black eyes with a touch of brown. The hair of his head was long and thick, straight or slightly curled. His beard also was thick, and he had a thin line of fine hair on his neck and chest. His cheeks were spare, his mouth large, and he had a pleasant smile. In complexion he was fair. He always walked as if he was rushing downhill, and others had difficulty in keeping up with him. When he turned in any direction, he did so with his whole body.

He was given to sadness, and there were long periods of silence when he was deep in thought; yet he never rested but was always busy with something. He never spoke unnecessarily. What he said was always to the point and sufficient to make his meaning clear, but there was no padding. From the first to last he spoke rapidly. Over his feelings he had a firm control. When he was annoyed he would turn aside; when he was pleased, he lowered his eyes. His time was carefully apportioned according to the various demands on him. In his dealings with people he was above all tactful. He could be severe at times, though in the main he was not rough but gentle. His laugh was mostly a smile.

Of the many stories illustrating his gentleness and tenderness of feeling, some at least are worthy of credence. The widow of his cousin Ja'far ibn-Abī-Ṭālib herself told her grand-daughter how he broke the news of Ja'far's death. She had been busy one morning with her household duties, which had included tanning forty hides and kneading dough, when Muhammad called. She collected her children – she had three sons by Ja'far – washed their faces and anointed them. When Muhammad entered, he asked for the sons of Ja'far. She brought them, and Muhammad put his arms round them and smelt them, as a mother would a baby. Then his eyes filled with tears and he burst out weeping. 'Have you heard something about Ja'far?' she asked, and he told her he had been killed. Later he instructed some of his people to prepare food for Ja'far's household, 'for they are too busy today to think about themselves.'

He seems to have been specially fond of children and to have got on well with them. Perhaps it was the yearning of a man who saw all his sons die as infants. Much of his paternal affection went to his adopted son Zayd. He was also attached to his younger cousin 'Alī ibn-Abī-Ṭālib, who had been a member of his household for a time; but he doubtless realized that 'Alī had not the makings of a successful statesman. For a time a grand-daughter called Umāmah was a favourite. He would carry her on his shoulder during the public prayers, setting her down when he bowed or prostrated, then picking her up again. On one occasion he teased his wives by showing them a necklace and saying he would give it to the one who was dearest to him; when he thought their feelings were sufficiently agitated, he presented it not to any of them, but to Umāmah.

He was able to enter into the spirit of childish games and had many friends among children. He had fun with the children who came back from Abyssinia and spoke Abyssinian. In one house in Medina there was a small boy with whom he was accustomed to have jokes. One day he found the small boy looking very sad, and asked what was the matter. When he was told that his pet nightingale had died, he did what he could to comfort him. His kindness extended even to animals, which is remarkable for Muhammad's century and part of the world. As his men marched towards Mecca just before the conquest they passed a bitch with puppies; and Muhammad not merely gave orders that they were not to be disturbed, but posted a man to see that the orders were carried out.

These are interesting sidelights on the personality of Muhammad, and fill out the picture formed of him from his conduct of public affairs. He gained men's respect and confidence by the religious basis of his activity and by qualities such as courage, resoluteness, impartiality and firmness inclining to severity but tempered by generosity. In addition to these he had a charm of manner which won their affection and secured their devotion.

Of all the world's great men none has been so much maligned as Muhammad. We saw above how this has come about. For centuries Islam was the great enemy of Christendom, since Christendom was in direct contact with no other organized states comparable in power to the Muslims. The Byzantine empire, after losing some of its best provinces to the Arabs, was being attacked in Asia Minor, while Western Europe was threatened through Spain and Sicily. Even before the Crusades focused attention on the expulsion of the Saracens from the Holy Land, medieval Europe was building up a conception of 'the great enemy.' At one point Muhammad was transformed into Mahound, the prince of darkness. By the twelfth century the ideas about Islam and Muslims current in the crusading armies were such travesties that they had a bad effect on morale. Practical considerations thus combined with scholarly zeal to foster the study matter and dissemination of more accurate information about Muhammad and his religion.

Since that time much has been achieved, especially during the last two centuries, but many of the old prejudices linger on. Yet in the modern world, where contacts between Christians and Muslims are closer than ever before, it is urgent that both should strive to reach an objective view of Muhammad's character. The denigration of him by

European writers has too often been followed by a romantic idealization of his figure by other Europeans and by Muslims. Neither denigration nor idealization is an adequate basis for the mutual relations of nearly half the human race. We are now back at the questions with which we began. We have an outline of the facts on which ultimate judgements must be based. What are our ultimate judgements to be?

One of the common allegations against Muhammad is that he was an impostor, who to satisfy his ambition and his lust propagated religious teachings which he himself knew to be false. Such insincerity, it was argued above (p. 17), makes the development of the Islamic religion incomprehensible. This point was first vigorously made over a hundred years ago by Thomas Carlyle in his lectures On Heroes, and it has since been increasingly accepted by scholars. Only a profound belief in himself and his mission explains Muhammad's readiness to endure hardship and persecution during the Meccan period when from a secular point of view there was no prospect of success. Without sincerity how could he have won the allegiance and even devotion of men of strong and upright character like Abī-Bakr and 'Umar? For the theist there is the further question how God could have allowed a great religion like Islam to develop on a basis of lies and deceit. There is thus a strong case for holding that Muhammad was sincere. If in some respects he was mistaken, his mistakes were not due to deliberate lying or imposture.

The other main allegations of moral defect in Muhammad are that he was treacherous and lustful. These are supported by reference to events like the violation of the sacred month on the expedition of Nakhlah (624) and his marriage to Zaynab bint-Jaḥsh, the divorced wife of his adopted son. About the bare facts there is no dispute, but it is not so clear that the facts justify the allegations. Was the violation of the sacred month an act of treachery or a justified breach with a piece of pagan religion? Was the marriage with Zaynab a yielding to sexual desire or a mainly political act in which an undesirable practice of 'adoption' belonging to a lower moral level was ended? Sufficient has been said above about the interpretation of these events to show that the case against Muhammad is much weaker than is sometimes thought.

The discussions of these allegations, however, raises a fundamental question. How are we to judge Muhammad? By the standards of his own time and country? Or by those of the most enlightened opinion in the West today? When the sources are closely scrutinized, it is clear that those of Muhammad's actions which are disapproved by the modern West were not the object of the *moral* criticism of his contemporaries. They criticized some of his acts, but their motives were superstitious prejudice or fear of the consequences. If they criticized the events at Nakhlah, it was because they feared some punishment from the offended pagan gods or the worldly vengeance of the Meccans. If they were amazed at the mass execution of the Jews of the clan of Qurayẓah, it was at the number and danger of the blood-feuds incurred. The marriage with Zaynab seemed incestuous, but this conception of incest was bound up with old practices belonging to a lower, communalistic level of familial institutions where a child's paternity was not definitely known; and this lower level was in process of being eliminated by Islam.

From the standpoint of Muhammad's time, then, the allegations of treachery and sensuality cannot be maintained. His' contemporaries did not find him morally defective in any way. On the contrary, some of the acts criticized by the modern Westerner show that Muhammad's standards were higher than those of his time. In his day and generation he was a social reformer, even a reformer in the sphere of morals. He created a new system of social security and a new family structure, both of which were a vast improvement on what went before. By taking what was best in the morality of the nomad and adapting it for settled communities, he established a religious and social framework for the life of many races of men. That is not the work of a traitor or 'an old lecher.'

It is sometimes asserted that Muhammad's character declined after he went to Medina, but there are no solid grounds for this view. It is based on too facile a use of the principle that all power corrupts and absolute power corrupts absolutely. The allegations of moral defects are attached to incidents belonging to the Medinan and not the Meccan period; but according to the interpretation of these incidents given in this book they marked no failure in Muhammad to live up to his ideals and no lapse from his moral principles. The persecuted preacher of Mecca was no less a man of his time than the ruler of Medina. If nothing is recorded of the preacher to show us how different his attitude was from that of nineteenth-century Europe, it does not follow that his ideals were any loftier (by our standards) than those of the reforming ruler. The opposite is more likely to be the case, since the preacher was nearer to the pagan background. In both Meccan and Medinan periods Muhammad's contemporaries looked on him as a good and upright man, and in the eyes of history he is a moral and social reformer.

So much must be said in fairness to Muhammad when he is measured against the Arabs of his time. Muslims, however, claim that he is a model of conduct and character for all mankind. In so doing they present him for judgement according to the standards of enlightened world opinion. Though the world is increasingly becoming one world, it has so far paid scant attention to Muhammad as a moral exemplar. Yet because Muslims are numerous, it will sooner or later have to consider seriously whether from the life and teaching of Muhammad any principles are to be learnt which will contribute to the moral development of mankind.

To this question no final answer has yet been given. What has been said so far by Muslims in support of their claims for Muhammad is but a preliminary statement and has convinced few non-Muslims. It is still open to the Muslims of today, however, to give the rest of the world a fuller and better presentation of their case. Will they be able to sift the universal from the particular in the life of Muhammad and so discover moral principles which make a creative contribution to the present world situation? Or, if this is too much to expect, will they at least be able to show that Muhammad's life is one possible exemplification of the ideal for all humanity? If they make a good case, some Christians will be ready to listen to them and to learn whatever is to be learned.

In this enterprise the difficulties confronting Muslims are immense. A combination of sound scholarship and deep moral insight is needed, and this combination is rare. My personal view is that Muslims are unlikely to be successful in their attempt to influence world opinion, at least in the sphere of morals. In the wider sphere of religion they have probably something to contribute to the world, for they have retained emphases – on the reality of God, for example –which have been neglected or forgotten in important sections of the other monotheistic religions; and I for one gladly acknowledge my indebtedness to the writings of men like al-Ghazālī. But towards convincing Christian Europe that Muhammad is the ideal man little, indeed nothing, has so far been accomplished.

Circumstances of time and place favoured Muhammad. Various forces combined to set the stage for his life-work and for the subsequent expansion of Islam. There was the social unrest in Mecca and Medina, the movement towards monotheism, the reaction against Hellenism in Syria and Egypt, the decline of the Persian and Byzantine empires, and a growing realization by the nomadic Arabs of the opportunities for plunder in the settled lands round them. Yet these forces, and others like them which might be added, would not in themselves account for the rise of the empire known as the Umayyad caliphate nor for the development of Islam into a world religion. There was nothing inevitable or automatic about the spread of the Arabs and the growth of the Islamic community. Without a remarkable combination of qualities in Muhammad it is improbable that the expansion would have taken place, and the military potential of the Arabs might easily have spent itself in raids on Syria and 'Irāq with no lasting consequences. These qualities fall into three groups.

First there is Muhammad's gift as a seer. Through him –or, on the orthodox Muslim view, through the revelations made to him – the Arab world was given a framework of ideas within which the resolution of its social tensions became possible. The provision of such a framework involved both insight into the fundamental causes of the social malaise of the time, and the genius to express this insight in a form which would stir the hearer to the depths of his being. The European reader may be 'put off' by the Qur'ān, but it was admirably suited to the needs and conditions of the day.

Secondly, there is Muhammad's wisdom as a statesman. The conceptual structure found in the Qur'ān was merely a framework. The framework had to support a building of concrete policies and concrete institutions. In the course of this book much has been said about Muhammad's far-sighted political strategy and his social reforms. His wisdom in these matters is shown by the rapid expansion of his small state to a world-empire after his death, and by the adaptation of his social institutions to many different environments and their continuance for thirteen centuries.

Thirdly, there is his skill and tact as an administrator and his wisdom in the choice of men to whom to delegate administrative details. Sound institutions and a sound policy will not go far if the execution of affairs is faulty and fumbling. When Muhammad died, the state he had founded was a 'going concern,' able to withstand the shock of his removal and, once it had recovered from this shock, to expand at prodigious speed.

The more one reflects on the history of Muhammad and of early Islam, the more one is amazed at the vastness of his achievement. Circumstances presented him with an opportunity such as few men have had, but the man was fully matched with the hour. Had it not been for his gifts as seer, statesman, and administrator and, behind these, his trust in God and firm belief that God had sent him, a notable chapter in the history of mankind would have remained unwritten.

So far Muhammad has been described from the point of view of the historian. Yet as the founder of a world-religion he also demands a theological judgement. Emil Brunner, for example, considers his claim to be a prophet, holds that it 'does not seem to be in any way justified by the actual content of the revelations,' but admits that, 'had Mohammed been a pre-Christian prophet of Arabia, it would not be easy to exclude him from the ranks of the messengers who prepared the way for the revelation.' Without presuming to enter into the theological complexities behind Brunner's view, I shall try, at the level of the educated man who has no special knowledge of either Christian or Islamic theology, to put forward some general considerations relevant to the question.

I would begin by asserting that there is found, at least in some men, what may be called 'creative imagination.' Notable instances are artists, poets and imaginative writers. All these put into sensuous form (pictures, poems, dramas, novels) what many are feeling but are unable to express fully. Great works of the creative imagination have thus a certain universality, in that they give expression to the feelings and attitudes of a whole generation. They are, of course, not imaginary, for they deal with real things; but they employ images, visual or conjured up by words, to express what is beyond the range of man's intellectual conceptions.

Prophets and prophetic religious leaders, I should maintain, share in this creative imagination. They proclaim ideas connected with what is deepest and most central in human experience, with special reference to the particular needs of their day and generation. The mark of the great prophet is the profound attraction of his ideas for those to whom they are addressed.

Where do such ideas come from? Some would say 'from the unconscious.' Religious people say 'from God,' at least with regard to the prophets of their own tradition, though a few would go so far as to claim with Baron Friedrich von Hügel, 'that everywhere there is some truth; that this truth comes originally from God.' Perhaps it could be maintained that these ideas of the creative imagination come from that life in a man which is greater than himself and is largely below the threshold of consciousness. For the Christian this still implies some connexion with God, for, according to Saint John, in the Word was life, and Jesus said 'I am the Life.'

The adoption of one of these views does not settle all the questions at issue. What about those ideas of the creative imagination which are false or unsound? Baron von Hügel is careful to say only that truth comes from God. Religious tradition has also held that ideas might come from the devil. Even if the creative imagination is an instrument which may be used by God or Life, that does not necessarily imply that all its ideas are true or sound. In Adolf Hitler the creative imagination was well developed, and his ideas had a wide appeal, but it is usually held that he was neurotic and that those Germans who followed him most devotedly became infected by his neurosis.

In Muhammad, I should hold, there was a welling up of the creative imagination, and the ideas thus produced are to a great extent true and sound. It does not follow, however, that all the Qur'ānic ideas are true and sound. In particular there is at least one point at which they seem to be unsound – the idea that 'revelation' or the product of the creative imagination is superior to normal human traditions as a source of bare historical fact. There are several verses in the Qur'ān (11. 51; 3. 39; 12. 103) to the effect that this is one of the reports of the unseen which We reveal to thee; thou didst not know it, thou nor thy people, before this One could admit a claim that the creative imagination was able to give a new and truer interpretation of a historical event, but to make it a source of bare fact is an exaggeration and false.

This point is of special concern to Christians, since the Qur'ān denies the bare fact of the death of Jesus on the cross, and Muslims still consider that this denial outweighs the contrary testimony of historical tradition. The primary intention of the Qur'ān was to deny the Jews' interpretation of the crucifixion as a victory for themselves, but as normally explained it goes much farther. The same exaggeration of the role of 'revelation' has also had other consequences. The Arab contribution to Islamic culture has been unduly magnified, and that of the civilized peoples of Egypt, Syria, 'Irāq and Persia, later converted to Islam, has been sadly belittled.

Too much must not be made of this slight flaw. Which of us, conscious of being called by God to perform a special task, would not have been more than a little proud? On the whole Muhammad was remarkably free from pride. Yet this slight exaggeration of his own function has had grave consequences and cannot be ignored.

Finally, what of our question? Was Muhammad a prophet? He was a man in whom creative imagination worked at deep levels and produced ideas relevant to the central questions of human existence, so that his religion has had a widespread appeal, not only in his own age but in succeeding centuries. Not all the ideas he proclaimed are true and sound, but by God's grace he has been enabled to provide millions of men with a better religion than they had before they testified that there is no god but God and that Muhammad is the messenger of God.

VI

HISTORY OF THE ARABS: FROM THE EARLIEST TIMES TO THE PRESENT

THOUGH the only one of the world prophets to be born within the full light of history, Muhammad is but little known to us in his early life: of his struggle for a livelihood, his efforts towards self-fulfilment and his gradual and painful realization of the great task awaiting him we have but few reliable reports... In his call and message the Arabian Muhammad was as truly prophetic as any of the Hebrew prophets of the Old Testament. God is one. He is all-powerful. He is the creator of the universe. There is a judgment day. Splendid rewards in Paradise await those who carry out God's commands, and terrible punishment in hell for those who disregard them. Such was the gist of his early message.

Consecrated and fired by the new task which he felt called upon to perform as the messenger (rasūl) of Allah, Muhammad now went among his own people teaching, preaching, delivering the new message. They laughed him to scorn. He turned nadhīr (Koran 67 : 26; 51 : 50, 51), warner, prophet of doom, seeking to effect his purpose by vivid and thrilling description of the joys of Paradise and the terrors of hell, even threatening his hearers with imminent doom. Short, crisp, expressive and impressive were his early revelations, the Makkan sūrahs.

As glorifier of his Lord, admonisher to his people, messenger and prophet (nabi) of Allah, Muhammad was gaining few converts... But abu-Sufyān, representing the aristocratic and influential Umayyad branch of Quraysh, stood adamant. What they considered a heresy seemed to run counter to the best economic interests of the Quraysh as custodians of al-Kaʿbah, the pantheon of multitudinous deities and centre of a pan-Arabian pilgrimage.

As new recruits, mainly from among the slave and lower classes, began to swell the ranks of the believers, the ridicule and sarcasm which had hitherto been used unsparingly on the part of the Quraysh were no longer deemed effective as weapons; it became necessary to resort to active persecution. These new measures resulted in the migration to Abyssinia of eleven Makkan families followed in 615 by some eighty-three others, chief among whom was that of ʿUthmān ibn-ʿAffān. The émigrés found asylum in the domain of the Christian Negus, who was unbending in his refusal to deliver them into the hands of their oppressors. Undaunted through these dark days of persecution by the temporary loss of so many followers, Muhammad fearlessly continued to preach and by persuasion convert men from the worship of the many and false gods to that of the one and true God, Allah. The revelations did not cease to "descend"...

Within this pre-Hijrah period there also falls the dramatic isrā,[1] that nocturnal journey in which the Prophet is said to have been instantly transported from al-Kaʿbah to Jerusalem preliminary to his ascent (miʾrāj) to the seventh heaven. Since it thus served as the terrestrial station on this memorable journey, Jerusalem, already sacred to the Jews and Christians, has become and remained the third holiest city after Makkah and al-Madīnah in the Moslem world...

About 620 some Yathribites, mainly of the Khazraj tribe, met Muhammad at the ʿUkāz fair and grew interested in what he had to say. Two years later a deputation of about seventy-five men invited him to make Yathrib (al-Madīnah) his home, hoping thereby to secure a means for reconciling the hostile Aws and Khazraj. In al-Madīnah the Jews, who were looking forward to a Messiah, had evidently

45

predisposed their heathen compatriots in favour of such a claimant as Muhammad. Having paid a futile propagandist visit to al-Taif and believing his cause lost in his native town, Muhammad allowed two hundred followers to elude the vigilance of the Quraysh and slip quietly into al-Madīnah, his mother's native city; he himself followed and arrived there on September 24, 622. Such was the famous hegira (hijrah) – not entirely a "flight" but a scheme of migration carefully considered for some two years. Seventeen years later the Caliph 'Umar designated that lunar year (beginning July 16) in which the Hijrah took place as the official starting-point of the Moslem era.

The Hijrah, with which the Makkan period ended and the Madīnese period began, proved a turning-point in the life of Muhammad. Leaving the city of his birth as a despised prophet, he entered the city of his adoption as an honoured chief...

In 628 Muhammad led a body of 1400 believers to the city of his birth and exacted the pact of al-Ḥudaybiyah, in which Makkans and Moslems were treated on equal terms. This treaty practically ended the war of Muhammad with his people, the Quraysh. Among other members of this tribe, Khālid ibn-al-Walīd and 'Amr ibn-al-'Āsi), destined to become the two mighty swords of militant Islam, were about this time received as recruits to the great cause. Two years later, towards the end of January 630 (AH 8), the conquest of Makkah was complete. Entering its great sanctuary Muhammad smashed the many idols, said to have numbered three hundred and sixty, exclaiming: "Truth hath come, and falsehood hath vanished!" The people themselves, however, were treated with special magnanimity. Hardly a triumphal entry in ancient annals is comparable to this.

In AH 9 Muhammad stationed a garrison at Tabūk, on the frontier of Ghassānland, and without a single engagement concluded treaties of peace with the Christian chief of Aylah (al-'Aqabah) and the Jewish tribes in the oases of Maqna, Adhruh and al-Jarbā to the south. The native Jews and Christians were taken under the protection of the newly arising Islamic community in consideration of a payment later called jizyah. This act set a precedent far-reaching in its consequences.

This year 9 (630–31) is called the "year of delegations" (sanat al-wufūd). During it delegations flocked from near and far to offer allegiance to the prince-prophet. Tribes joined out of convenience if not conviction, and Islam contented itself with exacting a verbal profession of faith and a payment of zakāh (poor tax). The large number of Bedouins who joined the new order may be surmised from a saying attributed to 'Umar, "The Bedouins are the raw material of Islam." Tribes and districts which had sent no representatives before sent them now. They came from distant 'Umān, Ḥaḍramawt and al-Yaman. The Ṭayyi' sent deputies and so did the Hamdān and Kindah. Arabia, which had hitherto never bowed to the will of one man, seemed now inclined to be dominated by Muhammad and be incorporated into his new scheme. Its heathenism was yielding to a nobler faith and a higher morality.

In the tenth Moslem year Muhammad entered triumphantly at the head of the annual pilgrimage into his new religious capital, Makkah. This proved his last visit and was therefore styled "the farewell pilgrimage." Three months after his return to al-Madīnah, he unexpectedly took ill and died complaining of severe headache on June 8, 632.

To the Madīnese period in the life of the Prophet belong the lengthy and more verbose sūrahs of the Koran which contain, in addition to the religious laws governing fasting and almsgiving and prayer, social and political ordinances dealing with marriage and divorce and the treatment of slaves, prisoners of war and enemies. On behalf of the slave, the orphan, the weak and the oppressed we find the legislation of him who was himself once a poor orphan especially benevolent.

Even in the height of his glory Muhammad led, as in his days of obscurity, an unpretentious life in one of those clay houses consisting, as do all old-fashioned houses of present-day Arabia and Syria, of a few rooms opening into a courtyard and accessible only therefrom. He was often seen mending his own clothes and was at all times within the reach of his people. The little he left he regarded as state property. Some for love, others for political reasons, he took about a dozen wives, among whom his favourite was 'Āishah, the young daughter of abu-Bakr. By Khadijah he had a number of children, none of whom survived him except Fāṭimah, the famous spouse of 'Ali. Muhammad mourned bitterly the loss of his infant son Ibrāhīm, born to him by

Mary, a Christian Copt. "Serious or trivial, his daily behaviour has instituted a canon which millions observe at this day with conscious mimicry. No one regarded by any section of the human race as Perfect Man has been imitated so minutely."[2]

Out of the religious community of al-Madīnah the later and larger state of Islam arose. This new community of Emigrants and Supporters was established on the basis of religion as the Ummat (congregation of) Allah. This was the first attempt in the history of Arabia at a social organization with religion, rather than blood, as its basis. Allah was the personification of state supremacy. His Prophet, as long as he lived, was His legitimate vicegerent and supreme ruler on earth. As such, Muhammad, in addition to his spiritual function, exercised the same temporal authority that any chief of a state might exercise. All within this community, regardless of tribal affiliation and older loyalties, were now brethren at least in principle. These are the words of the Prophet in his noble sermon at the "farewell pilgrimage":

> O ye men! harken unto my words and take ye them to heart! Know ye that every Moslem is a brother unto every other Moslem, and that ye are now one brotherhood. It is not legitimate for any one of you, therefore, to appropriate unto himself anything that belongs to his brother unless it is willingly given him by that brother.

Thus by one stroke the most vital bond of Arab relationship, that of tribal kinship, was replaced by a new bond, that of faith; a sort of Pax Islamica was instituted for Arabia. The new community was to have no priesthood, no hierarchy, no central see. Its mosque was its public forum and military drill ground as well as its place of common worship. The leader in prayer, the imām, was also to be commander in chief of the army of the faithful, who were enjoined to protect one another against the entire world. All Arabians who remained heathen were outside the pale, almost outlaws. Islam cancelled the past. Wine (khamr, from Aramaic) and gambling – next to women the two indulgences dearest to the Arabian heart – were abolished in one verse.[3] Singing, almost equally attractive, was frowned upon. This contrast between the old order and the new was vividly drawn by the apocryphal words put in the mouth of Ja'far ibn-abi-Ṭalib, the spokesman of the Moslem emigrants to Abyssinia. Said Ja'far to the Negus:

> Jāhilīyah people were we, worshipping idols, feeding on dead animals [maytah],[4] practising immorality, deserting our families and violating the covenant terms of mutual protection, with the strong among us devouring the weak. Such was our state until Allah sent unto us a messenger from amongst ourselves whose ancestry we know and whose veracity, fidelity and purity we recognize. He it was who summoned us to Allah in order to profess Him as one and worship Him alone, discarding whatever stones and idols we and our forbears before us worshipped in His stead. He moreover commanded us to be truthful in our talk, to render to others what is due them, to stand by our families and to refrain from doing wrong and shedding blood. He forbade committing fornication, bearing false witness, depriving the orphan of his legitimate right and speaking ill of chaste women. He enjoined on us the worship of Allah alone, associating with Him no other. He also ordered us to observe prayer, pay zakāh [alms] and practise fasting.[5]

Within a brief span of mortal life Muhammad called forth out of unpromising material a nation never united before, in a country that was hitherto but a geographical expression; established a religion which in vast areas superseded Christianity and Judaism and still claims the adherence of a goodly portion of the human race; and laid the basis of an empire that was soon to embrace within its far-flung boundaries the fairest provinces of the then civilized world. Himself an unschooled man, Muhammad was nevertheless responsible for a book still considered by one-eighth of mankind as the embodiment of all science, wisdom and theology.

The charge of corrupting history, in the cause of religion, has been always committed to the most famous champions, and greatest saints of each church; and, if I was not more afraid of tiring, than of scandalising your lordship, I could quote to you examples of modern churchmen who have endeavored to justify foul language by the New Testament, and cruelty by the Old... In other cases this charge belongs to the pedants of every nation, and the tools of every party. What accusations of idolatry and superstition have not been brought, and aggravated against the Mahometans? Those wretched Christians who returned from those wars, so improperly called the holy wars, rumored these stories about the West; and you may find, in some of the old chroniclers and romance writers, as well as poets, the Saracens called Paynims; though surely they were much further off from any suspicion of polytheism, than those who called them by that name. When Mahomet the Second took Constantinople in the fifteenth century, the Mahometans began to be a little better, and but a little better known, than they had been before, to these parts of the world. But their religion, as well as their customs and manners, was strangely misrepresented by the Greek refugees that fled from the Turks: and the terror and hatred which this people had inspired by the rapidity of their conquests, and by their ferocity, made all these misrepresentations universally pass for truths. Many such instances may be collected from Maraccio's refutation of the Koran, and Relandus has published a very valuable treatise on purpose to refute these calumnies, and to justify the Mahometans.

JOHN L. ESPOSITO

VII

MUHAMMAD:
PROPHET OF GOD

HISTORY, legend, and Muslim belief portray Muhammad as a remarkable man and prophet. While we know a good deal about Muhammad's life after his "call" to be God's messenger, historical records tell us little about Muhammad's early years prior to becoming a prophet at the age of forty in 610 CE. The Quran has served as a major source for information regarding the life of the Prophet. In addition, Prophetic traditions (reports about what Muhammad said and did) and biographies give us a picture of his meaning and significance in early Islam as do Islamic calligraphy and art, where the names of Allah and Muhammad often occur side by side – God and His Prophet. Muhammad) serves both as God's human instrument in bearing His revelation and as the model or ideal whom all believers should emulate. Thus, under standing Muhammad and his role in the early Islamic community is crucial for an appreciation of the development of early Islam as well as the dynamics of contemporary Muslim belief and practice.

Muhammad ibn Abdullah (the son of Abd Allah) was born in

570. Tradition tells us that he was orphaned at a young age. His father was a trader who died before Muhammad was born; his mother, Amina, died when he was only six years old. As a young man, Muhammad was employed in Mecca's thriving caravan trade. The city was at the crossroads of trade routes between the Indian Ocean and the Mediterranean. Central Arabia was emerging as a major commercial power, sitting astride important trade routes that extended from Africa across the Middle East to China and Malaysia. Muhammad became a steward or business manager for the caravans of a wealthy widow, Khadija, whom he subsequently married. Tradition tells us that at the time, Muhammad was twenty-five years old and Khadija was forty. During their fifteen years of marriage, they enjoyed a very close relationship and had three sons (who died in infancy) and four daughters. The most famous of Muhammad's surviving children was Fatima, who would marry Ali, the revered fourth caliph of Sunni Islam and the first legitimate *Imam* (leader) of Shii Islam.

Mecca was a prosperous center of trade and commerce. Yet it was a society in which traditional tribal ways were strained by Mecca's transition from a semi-Bedouin to a commercial, urban society. This process was accompanied by serious economic and social cleavages. Muhammad, who had become a successful member of Meccan society, was apparently profoundly affected by these changes. He enjoyed great respect for his judgment and trustworthiness, as was reflected by his nickname al-Amin, the trusted one. This rectitude was complemented by a reflective nature that led him to retreat regularly to a cave on Mt. Hira, a few miles north of Mecca. Here, in long periods of solitude, he contemplated his life and the ills of his society, seeking greater meaning and insight. Here, at the age of forty during the month of Ramadan, Muhammad the caravan leader became Muhammad the messenger of God. On the night Muslims call "The Night of Power and Excellence," he received the first of many revelations from God. A heavenly intermediary, later identified by tradition as the angel Gabriel, commanded, "Recite." Muhammad responded that he had nothing to recite. Twice the angel repeated the command, and each time a frightened and bewildered Muhammad pleaded that he did not know what to say. Finally, the words came to him:

Muhammad: Prophet of God

Recite in the name of your Lord who has created, Created man out of a germ-cell. Recite for your Lord is the Most Generous One Who has taught by the pen, Taught man what he did not know!

With this revelation, Muhammad joined that group of individuals whom Semitic faiths acknowledge as divinely inspired messengers or prophets of God. Muhammad continued to receive divine revelations over a period of twenty-two years (610–632). These messages were finally collected and written down in the Quran ("The Recitation"), Islam's sacred scripture.

Muslim tradition reports that Muhammad reacted to his "call" in much the same way as the Hebrew prophets. He was both frightened and reluctant. Frightened by the unknown – for surely he did not expect such an experience. Reluctant, at first, because he feared he was possessed and that others would dismiss his claims as inspired by spirits, or jinns. Despondent and confused, Muhammad resolved to kill himself but was stopped when he again heard the voice say, "O Muhammad! You are the messenger of God and I am Gabriel." This message was reinforced by his wife, Khadija, who reassured him that he was neither mad nor possessed; the messenger was from God and not a demon. Interestingly, according to Muslim tradition a Christian played an important role as well. One of those to whom Khadija and Muhammad turned for advice was her Christian cousin, Waraqa ibn Qusayy. When he heard of Muhammad's experience, Waraqa reassured him:

Surely, by Him in whose hand is Waraqa's soul, thou art the prophet of this people. There hath come unto thee the greatest Namus (angel or Gabriel) who came unto Moses. Like the Hebrew prophets, Thou wilt be called a liar, and they will use thee despitefully and cast thee out and fight against thee.[1]

For just such reasons, Muhammad, like many of the prophets before him, was initially reluctant to preach God's message. His fears were well-founded.

The first ten years of Muhammad's preaching were difficult, marked by Meccan resistance and rejection. While there was a trickle of converts, opposition to Muhammad was formidable. For the powerful and prosperous Meccan oligarchy, the monotheistic message of this would- be reformer, with its condemnation of the socioeconomic inequities of Meccan life, constituted a direct challenge not only to traditional polytheistic religion but also to the power and prestige of the establishment, threatening their economic, social, and political interests. The Prophet denounced false contracts, usury, and the neglect and exploitation of orphans and widows. He defended the rights of the poor and the oppressed, asserting that the rich had an obligation to the poor and dispossessed. This sense of social commitment and responsibility was institutionalized in the form of religious tithes or taxes on wealth and agricultural lands. Like Amos and Jeremiah before him, Muhammad was a "warner" from God who admonished his hearers to repent and obey God, for the final judgment was near:

> Say: "O men, I am only for you a warner." Those who believe, and do deeds of righteousness – theirs shall be forgiveness and generous provision. And those who strive against Our signs to avoid them – they shall be inhabitants of Hell. (Quran 22:49–50)

Muhammad's rejection of polytheism undermined the religious prestige of the Meccans (in particular, the Umayyad clan) as keepers of the Kaba, the religious shrine that housed the tribal idols. It threatened the considerable revenues that accrued from the annual pilgrimage and festival to this central sanctuary of Arabian tribal religion. This potential economic loss was coupled with the undermining of Meccan tribal political authority by Muhammad's claim to prophetic authority and leadership and his insistence that all true believers belonged to a single universal community (*umma*) that transcended tribal bonds.

Creation of the Islamic Community

For almost ten years, Muhammad struggled in Mecca, preaching God's message and gathering a small band of faithful followers. Among the early converts were Ali, his cousin and son-in-law, and Abu Bakr, his future father-in-law and the first caliph, or successor of the Prophet.

Muhammad: Prophet of God

The deaths of Khadija and of his uncle and protector, Abu Talib, in 619 made life even more difficult. Meccan opposition escalated from derision and verbal attacks to active persecution. The core of the opposition came from the Umayyad clan of the Quraysh tribe. As we shall see, their descendants, even after their later conversion to Islam, would continue to challenge the family of the Prophet. As conditions deteriorated in Mecca, Muhammad sent some of his followers to other areas, such as Christian Abyssinia, for safety. The situation changed significantly in 620. Muhammad was invited by a delegation from Yathrib (later called Medina), a city two hundred miles north of Mecca, to serve as a chief arbitrator or judge in a bitter feud between its Arab tribes. Muhammad and two hundred of his followers quietly emigrated, from July to September 622, to Medina. This migration (*hijra*) marked a turning point in Muhammad's fortunes and a new stage in the history of the Islamic movement. Islam took on political form with the establishment of an Islamic community-state at Medina. The importance of the *hijra* is reflected in its adoption as the beginning of the Islamic calendar. Muslims chose to date their history from neither Muhammad's birth nor his reception of the first revelation in 610, but from the creation of the Islamic community (*umma*). The community, as much as the individual, was to be the vehicle for realizing God's will on earth.

Muhammad at Medina

At Medina, Muhammad had the opportunity to implement God's governance and message, for he was now the prophet-head of a religiopolitical community. He did this by establishing his leadership in Medina, subduing Mecca, and consolidating Muslim rule over the remainder of Arabia through diplomatic and military means.

Muhammad had come to Medina as the arbiter or judge for the entire community, Muslim and non-Muslim alike. In addition, he was the leader of all the Muslims, the commander of the faithful, both those who had emigrated from Mecca and those raised in Medina. While the majority of the Arab tribes came to embrace Islam, the Jewish tribes (that is, those Arabs who had previously converted to Judaism) remained an important minority. Muhammad promulgated a charter, sometimes called the constitution of Medina, that set out the rights and duties of all citizens and the relationship of the Muslim community to other communities. Muslims constituted a community whose primary identity and bond were no longer to be tribal ties but a common religious faith and commitment. Jews were recognized as a separate community allied to the Muslim *umma*, but with religious and cultural autonomy.

As the Medinan state was taking shape, Muhammad turned his attention to Mecca. Mecca was the religious, political, economic, and intellectual center of Arabia. Its importance was not diminished by its hostility to Muhammad's preaching. If anything, further revelations to Muhammad, which designated Mecca as the direction (*qibla*) for prayer and the site for Muslim pilgrimage (*hajj*), increased its religious significance. Muslim religious fervor was matched by the power of Meccan tribal mores that branded the Muslims as secessionists and traitors. All the ingredients were there for a formidable battle. Muhammad initiated a series of raids against Meccan caravans, threatening both the political authority and the economic power of the Quraysh. Several important battles ensued. In 624 at Badr, near Medina, Muslim forces, though greatly outnumbered, defeated the Meccan army. For Muslims, then and now, the Battle of Badr has special significance. It was the first and a most decisive victory for the forces of monotheism over those of polytheism, for the army of God over the followers of ignorance and unbelief. God had sanctioned and assisted His soldiers (Quran 3:123, 8:42ff) in victory. Quranic witness to divine guidance and intervention made Badr a sacred symbol, and it has been used throughout Muslim history, as evidenced most recently in the 1973 Egyptian-Israeli war, whose Egyptian code name was "Operation Badr."

The elation after Badr was dissipated when Muslims were defeated by the Meccans in the Battle of Uhud in 625, in which Muhammad himself was wounded. Finally, in 627, frustrated by the growing strength of Muhammad, the Meccans mounted an all-out seige of Medina in order to crush their opposition once and for all. At the Battle of the "Ditch" (so named because the Muslims dug a trench to neutralize the Meccan cavalry), the Muslims held out so successfully against a coalition of Meccans and mercenary Bedouins that the coalition disintegrated. The Meccans withdrew. The failure of the Quraysh enhanced Muhammad's prestige and leadership among the tribes of Arabia, placing him in the ascendant position. He had consolidated his leadership in Medina, extended his influence over other tribal areas in the Hijaz, and asserted his independence of the dominant tribe in central Arabia. The balance of power had shifted. Muhammad would now initiate, and Mecca would respond.

The final phase in the struggle between Medina and Mecca highlights the method and political genius of Muhammad. He employed both military and diplomatic means, often preferring the latter. Instead of seeking to rout his Meccan opponents, Muhammad sought to gain submission to God and His messenger by incorporating them within the Islamic community-state. A truce was struck in 628 at Hudaybiyah to permit the Muslims to make their pilgrimage to Mecca the following year. In 629, Muhammad established Muslim control over the Hijaz and led the pilgrimage to Mecca, as had been scheduled. Then in 630, Muhammad accused the Quraysh of breaking the treaty, and the Muslims marched on Mecca, ten thousand strong. The Meccans capitulated. Eschewing vengeance and the plunder of conquest, the Prophet instead accepted a settlement, granting amnesty rather than wielding the sword toward his former enemies. For their part, the Meccans converted to Islam, accepted Muhammad's leadership, and were incorporated within the *umma*.

During the next two years, Muhammad established his authority over much of Arabia. The Bedouin who resisted were defeated militarily. At the same time, so many tribes in Arabia sent delegations to come to terms with the successor to the Quraysh that Muslim history remembers this period as the year of deputations. Alliances were forged. While many converted to Islam, others did not. Representatives were sent from Medina to teach the Quran and the duties and rituals of Islam, and to collect the taxes due Medina. In the spring of 632, Muhammad led the pilgrimage to Mecca, where the sixty-two-year-old leader preached his farewell sermon, exhorting his followers:

> Know ye that every Moslem is a brother unto every other Moslem, and that ye are now one brotherhood. It is not legitimate for any one of you,

therefore, to appropriate unto himself anything that belongs to his brother unless it is willingly given him by that brother.[2]

These words summarize both the nature of the Islamic community and the accomplishment of the Prophet Muhammad. When he died three months later in June 632, all Arabia was united under the banner of Islam.

Muhammad: Exemplar of Muslim Life and Piety

Muhammad was among those great religious figures, prophets and founders of religions, whose remarkable character and personality inspired uncommon confidence and commitment. His phenomenal success in attracting followers and creating a community-state that dominated Arabia could be attributed not only to the fact that he was a shrewd military strategist but also to the fact that he was an unusual man who elicited steadfast loyalty despite persecution and oppression. Muhammad's followers found him righteous, trustworthy, pious, compassionate, honest. He was revered from earliest times: Muslims remembered and recounted what he said and did. Both during his lifetime and throughout the following centuries, Muhammad has served as the ideal model for Muslim life, providing the pattern that all believers are to emulate. He is, as some Muslims say, the "living Quran" – the witness whose behavior and words reveal God's will. Thus the practices of the Prophet became a material source of Islamic law alongside the Quran.

Muslims look to Muhammad's example for guidance in all aspects of life: how to treat friends as well as enemies, what to eat and drink, how to make love and war. Nowhere is this seen more clearly than in the growth of Prophetic traditions. For the tribes of Arabia, the ideals and norms of their way of life had been contained and preserved in their practices (*sunna*, trodden path), the customs or oral laws handed down from previous generations by word and example. As Prophet and leader of the community, Muhammad reformed these practices. Old ways were modified, eliminated, or replaced by new regulations. His impact on Muslim life cannot be overestimated, since he served as both religious and political head of Medina: prophet of God, ruler, military commander, chief judge, lawgiver. As a result, the practice of the Prophet, his *Sunna* or example, became the norm for community life.

Muslims observed and remembered stories about what the Prophet said and did. These reports or traditions (*hadith*) were preserved and passed on in oral and written form. The corpus of *hadith* literature reveals the comprehensive scope of Muhammad's example; he is the ideal religiopolitical leader as well as the exemplary husband and father. Thus when many Muslims pray five times each day or make the pilgrimage to Mecca, they seek to pray as the Prophet prayed, without adding or subtracting from the way Muhammad is reported to have worshipped. Traditions of the Prophet provide guidance for personal hygiene, dress, eating, marriage, treatment of wives, diplomacy, and warfare.

Reformer

Muhammad was not the founder of Islam; he did not start a new religion. Like his prophetic predecessors, he came as a religious reformer. Muhammad maintained that he did not bring a new message from a new God but called people back to the one, true God and to a way of life that most of his contemporaries had forgotten or deviated from. Worship of Allah was not the evolutionary emergence of monotheism from polytheism but a return to a forgotten past, to the faith of the first monotheist, Abraham. The Prophet brought a revolution in Arabian life, a reformation that sought to purify and redefine its way of life. False, superstitious practices such as polytheism and idolatry were suppressed. Such beliefs were viewed as the worst forms of ingratitude or unbelief, for they contradicted and denied the unity or oneness (*tawhid*) of God. Polytheism, or association (*shirk*) of anything with Allah, was denounced as the worst of sins, idolatry. For Muhammad, the majority of Arabs lived in ignorance (*jahiliyya*) of Allah and His will as revealed to the prophets Adam, Abraham, Moses, and Jesus. Moreover, he believed that both the Jewish and the Christian communities had distorted God's original revelation to Moses and later to Jesus. Thus, Islam brought a reformation; it was the call once again to total surrender or submission (*islam*) to Allah and the implementation of His will as revealed in its complete form one final time to Muhammad, the last, or "seal," of the prophets. For Muhammad, Islam was not a new faith but the restoration of the true faith (*iman*), a process that required the reformation of an ignorant, deviant society. Repentance, or the heeding of God's warning, required turning away from the path of unbelief and turning toward or returning to the straight path (*sharia*) or law of God. This conversion required both individual and group submission to God. Muslims were not only individuals but also a community or brotherhood of believers. They were bound by a common faith and committed to the creation of a socially just society through the implementation of God's will – the establishment of the rule or kingdom of God on earth.

The example of the Prophet offers a paradigm and the basis for an ideology for the fusion of religion and state in Muslim experience. The early Islamic worldview provides a model both for the formation of a state and for protest and revolution. The world is seen as divided between the believers or the friends of God, who represent the forces of good, and the unbelievers (*kafirs*) and hypocrites, who are the allies of evil, the followers of Satan:

> God is the Protector of the believers; He brings them forth from darkness to the light. And the unbelievers – their protectors are the idols, that bring them forth from the light into the shadows; those are the inhabitants of the Fire, therein dwelling forever. (Quran 2:257–59)

> The believers fight in the way of God, and the unbelievers fight in the idol's way. Fight you therefore against the friends of Satan. (4:76)

The Muslims in Mecca were the oppressed and disinherited, struggling in an unbelieving society. The Quran compares their plight with that of Moses and the Israelites before them (Quran 28:4–5). Muslims were reminded that God is their refuge and helper:

> And remember when you were few and abased in the land, and were fearful that the people would snatch you away; but He gave you refuge, and confirmed you with His help. (8:26)

Muhammad: Prophet of God

Faced with persecution, Muslims, like Muhammad at Mecca, had two choices: emigration (*hijra*) and armed resistance (*jihad*). First, the true believers were expected to leave a godless society and establish a community of believers under God and His Prophet. Second, Muslims were permitted, indeed exhorted, to struggle against the forces of evil and unbelief, and if necessary sacrifice their lives, in order to establish God's rule:

> So let them fight in the way of God who sell the present life for the world to come; and whosoever fights in the way of God and is slain, or conquers, We shall bring him a mighty wage. (4:74)

God's preference is made even clearer a few verses later: "God has preferred in rank those who struggle with their possessions and their selves over the ones who sit at home" (4:95).

Those who wage war (*jihad*) for God engage in a religiopolitical act, a holy war. The God who commands this struggle against oppression and unbelief will assist His Muslim holy warriors as He did at the Battle of Badr, where, the Quran states, an unseen army of angels aided the Muslim army. These holy warriors (*mujahidin*) will be rewarded in this life with victory and the spoils of war. Those who fall in battle will be rewarded with eternal life as martyrs (*shahid*, witness) for the faith. The Arabic term for martyr comes from the same root ("witness") as the word for the confession or profession of faith, indicating that willingness to sacrifice all, even life itself, is the ultimate profession or eternal witness of faith. In this way, early Islamic history provides Muslims with a model and ideology for protest, resistance, and revolutionary change.

The reformist spirit of Islam affected religious ritual as well as politics and society. This process of adaptation or Islamization would characterize much of the development of Islam. While Islam rejected some beliefs and institutions and introduced others, the more common method was to reformulate or adapt existing practices to Islamic norms and values. Rituals such as the annual pilgrimage (*hajj*) and prayer (*salat*) were reinterpreted. The Kaba remained the sacred center, but it was no longer associated with the tribal idols which had been destroyed when Muhammad conquered Mecca. Instead, he rededicated it to Allah, for whom, Muslims believe, Abraham and Ismail had originally built the Kaba. Similarly, Arab pagan and Jewish prayer practices were adapted rather than totally replaced. Muslims, too, were to pray at fixed times each day. However, they would pray to Allah, facing Mecca and reciting the Quran. Initially, Muslims, like the Jews of Arabia, faced Jerusalem to pray. However, when the Jews did not accept Muhammad's prophetic claims, a new revelation directed Muhammad to shift the center of prayer to Mecca.

Muhammad introduced a new moral order in which the origin and end of all actions was not self or tribal interest but God's will. Belief in the Day of Judgment and resurrection of the body added a dimension of human responsibility and accountability that had been absent in Arabian religion. Tribal vengeance and retaliation were subordinated to a belief in a just and merciful creator and judge. A society based on tribal affiliation and man-made tribal law or custom was replaced by a religiously bonded community (*umma*) governed by God's law.

Muhammad and the West

Talk of Islam's new moral order and the normative nature that Muhammad's life had for Muslims seems to clash with Western perceptions of Islam. If Muslim tradition tended to mythify the Prophet, Western tradition too often has denigrated and vilified his memory. Two issues in particular – Muhammad's treatment of the Jews and his (polygynous) marriages – have proven popular stumbling blocks, or perhaps more accurately whipping posts, for Western critics and polemics.

In his early preaching, Muhammad had looked to the Jews and Christians of Arabia as natural allies whose faiths had much in common with Islam. He anticipated their acceptance and approval. When the Islamic community was established at Medina, Muslims, like the Jews, had faced Jerusalem to pray. However, the Jewish tribes, which had long lived in Medina and had political ties with the Quraysh, tended to resist both religious and political cooperation with the Muslims. They denied Muhammad's prophethood and message and cooperated with his Meccan enemies. While the constitution of Medina had granted them autonomy in internal religious affairs, political loyalty and allegiance were expected. Yet the Quran accuses the Jewish tribes of regularly breaking such pacts: "Why is it that whenever they make pacts, a group among them casts it aside unilaterally?" (2:100).

After each major battle, one of the Jewish tribes was accused and punished for such acts. Muslim perception of distrust, intrigue, and rejection on the part of the Jews led first to exile and later to warfare. After Badr, the Banu Qainuqa tribe and after the Battle of Uhud, the Banu Nadir, with their families and possessions, were expelled from Medina. After the Battle of the Ditch in 627, the Jews of the Banu Qurayza were denounced as traitors who had consorted with the Meccans. As was common in Arab (and, indeed, Semitic) practice, the men were massacred; the women and children were spared but enslaved. However, it is important to note that the motivation for such actions was political rather than racial or theological. Although the Banu Qurayza had remained neutral, they had also negotiated with the Quraysh. Moreover, the exiled Jewish clans had actively supported the Meccans. Muhammad moved decisively to crush the Jews who re-mained in-Medina, viewing them as a continued political threat to the consolidation of Muslim dominance and rule in Arabia.

One final point should be made. Muhammad's use of warfare in general was alien neither to Arab custom nor to that of the Hebrew prophets. Both believed that God had sanctioned battle with the enemies of the Lord. Biblical stories about the exploits of kings and prophets such as Moses, Joshua, Elijah, Samuel, Jehu, Saul, and David recount the struggles of a community called by God and the permissibility, indeed requirement, to take up arms when necessary against those who had defied God, and to fight "in the name of the Lord of hosts, the God of the armies of Israel."[3] Similarly, in speaking of the Israelite conquests, Moses recalls: "And I commanded you at that time, saying, 'The Lord your God has given you this land to possess... You shall not fear them; for it is the Lord your God who fights for you'" (Deuteronomy 3:18–22).

Muhammad's marriages have long provided another source of Western criticism of the moral character of the Prophet. A noted British author has observed:

No great religious leader has been so maligned as Muhammad. Attacked in the past as a heretic, an imposter, or a sensualist, it is still possible to find him referred to as "the false prophet." A modern German writer accuses Muhammad of sensuality, surrounding himself with young women. This man was not married until he was twenty-five years of age, then he and his wife lived in happiness and fidelity for twenty-four years, until her death when he was forty-nine. Only between the age of fifty and his death at sixty-two did Muhammad take other wives, only one of whom was a virgin, and most of them were taken for dynastic and political reasons. Certainly the Prophet's record was better than that head of the Church of England, Henry VIII.

In addressing the issue of Muhammad's polygynous marriages, it is important to remember several points. First, Semitic culture in general and Arab practice in particular permitted polygyny. It was common practice in Arabian society, especially among nobles and leaders. Though less common, polygyny was also permitted in biblical and even in postbiblical Judaism. From Abraham, David, and Solomon down to the reformation period, polygyny was practiced by some Jews. While Jewish law changed after the Middle Ages due to the influence of Christian rule, for Jews under Islamic rule, polygyny remained licit, though it was not extensively practiced.[4] Second, during the prime of his life, Muhammad remained married to one woman, Khadija. Third, it was only after her death that he took a number of wives. Fourth, Muhammad's use of the special dispensation from God to exceed the limit of four wives imposed by the Quran, occurred only after the death of Khadija. Moreover, most of the eleven marriages had political and social motives. As was customary for Arab chiefs, many were political marriages to cement alliances. Others were marriages to the widows of his companions who had fallen in combat and were in need of protection. Remarriage was difficult in a society that emphasized virgin marriages. Aisha was the only virgin that Muhammad married and the wife with whom he had the closest relationship. Fifth, as we shall see later, Muhammad's teachings and actions, as well as the Quranic message, improved the status of all women – wives, daughters, mothers, widows, and orphans.

Talk of the political and social motives behind many of the Prophet's marriages should not obscure the fact that Muhammad was attracted to women and enjoyed his wives. To deny this would contradict the Islamic outlook on marriage and sexuality, found in both revelation and Prophetic traditions, which emphasizes the importance of family and views sex as a gift from God to be enjoyed within the bonds of marriage. The many stories about Muhammad's concern and care for his wives reflect these values.

VIII

ISLAM: MUHAMMAD

MUHAMMAD was born about 570 in Mecca as a member of the Hashim clan of the Quraish, to which most of the notables of Mecca belonged. He lost his parents early (his father died before his birth) and he was brought up by his uncle, Abu Talib. Like most of his Meccan compatriots, he devoted himself to trade. After some successful journeys to Syria the young Muhammad, called *al-Amīn* for his reliability, married his employer, Khadija, who was his senior by several years. She bore him several children, among whom four daughters survived; all but one predeceased their father. Muhammad did not marry any other woman as long as Khadija was alive (she died when he was about fifty years old). This fact certainly does not support the prejudice commonly vented in the West, where he was regarded as extremely sensual due to his numerous later marriages, which particularly upset those who espoused the ideal of celibacy.

Muhammad liked to retire at times to meditate in a cave in Mt. Hira, and when he was about forty years old, he was overcome by visions and even more by voices. It took him some time to realize that it was an angelic voice that was entrusting him with a divine mandate. Sura 96 of the Koran contains the first such address, *iqra'* ("Read" or "Recite!") and thus points to the groundbreaking experience. Khadija faithfully supported her husband in the spiritual crises triggered by these experiences.

The first proclamations preached by Muhammad are dominated by one single thought: the nearing Day of Judgment. The terrible shock caused by the sudden approach of the Hour, the Day of Reckoning, and the resurrection is heralded by breathless short lines in sonorous rhymed prose. Close is this Hour. In a short while it will knock at the door and will stir up from heedlessness those who are embroiled in worldly affairs and who have forgotten God! Then they will have to face their Lord to give account of their sinful actions. Natural catastrophes will announce the Day of Judgment – earthquakes, fires, eclipses – as described in Sura 81 in unforgettable words:

When the sun shall be darkened,
when the stars shall be thrown down,
when the mountains shall be set moving,
when the pregnant camels shall be neglected,
when the savage beasts shall be mustered,
when the seas shall be set boiling,
when the souls shall be coupled,
when the buried infant shall be asked for what sin she
was slain,
when the scrolls shall be unrolled,
when heaven shall be stripped off,
when Hell shall be set blazing,
when Paradise shall be brought nigh,
then shall a soul know what it has produced.
(translated by A. J. Arberry)

At that hour Israfil will blow the trumpet; the dead will be resurrected in the body and, in complete confusion, will ask each other about their fate. Certain trials have to be faced, and finally the unbelievers and sinners will be dragged away by their feet and their forelocks. The Koranic descriptions of Judgment and Hell do not reach the fantastic descriptions of, for example, Christian apocalyptic writing. Later popular piety, however, could never get enough detail of all kinds of chastisement; of terrible pain in the fire; of stinking, hot, or dirty water; of the fruits of poisonous trees; and of various tortures.

But Muhammad learned that he was not only sent to threaten and blame, but also to bring good tidings: every pious man who lives according to God's order will enter Paradise where rivers of milk and honey flow in cool, fragrant gardens and virgin beloveds await him. Women and children too participate in the paradisial bliss. In its description of Paradise, so often attacked by Christian polemists because of its sensuality, the *Koran* is not much more colorful than were the sermons on this topic in the Eastern orthodox church.

The practical-minded Meccan merchants did not take Muhammad's message seriously; to them a corporeal resurrection seemed both impossible and ludicrous. To refute their doubts, the *Koran* brings forth numerous proofs for such a resurrection. First, it cannot be difficult for God, who has created the world out of nothing, to reunite the already existing parts and particles. Second, a revivication of the – apparently – dead desert after rainfall is a symbol of the quickening of human beings. This reasoning was used time and again in later didactic and mystical poetry: for those who have eyes to see, every spring proves the resurrection. Finally, human fertility and birth can be taken as signs of God's unlimited creative power: the growth of a fertilized egg into a perfect living being is certainly no less miraculous than the resurrection of the dead. Furthermore, the judgments meted out to sinful peoples of the past and the calamities that wiped out ancient nations should be proof enough of how God deals with sinners as well as with those who reject the prophets sent to them, thus contributing to their own annihilation.

As the creation and the Last Judgment are closely related to each other, it is logical that the Creator and the Lord of Doomsday must be one and the same. The belief in one God, without partners and without adjunct deities, forms the center of the revelation from an early moment onward. Sura 112 declares: "Say: God is One; God the Eternal: He did not beget and is not begotten, and no one is equal to

Him." This sura, which is nowadays used mainly to refute the Christian trinitarian dogma, was probably first directed against the ancient Arab concept of 'the daughters of Allah.' But the tauhīd, the acknowledgment of God's unity, was to remain the heart of Islam, in whichever way it was understood, and the only sin that cannot be forgiven is shirk, "associating something with God."

The duty of human beings is to surrender to this unique, omnipotent God, the Merciful, the Compassionate (as He is called at the beginning of each chapter of the Koran and also at the beginning of every human activity); to surrender from the bottom of one's heart, with one's whole soul and one's entire mind. The word "Islam" means this complete surrender to the Divine will; and the one who practices such surrender is a Muslim (active participle of the fourth stem of the root s.l.m., which has also the connotation of salām, "peace"). Muslims do not like the term "Muhammedan," as it suggests an incorrect parallel to the way Christians call themselves after Christ. Only members of some late mystical currents called themselves Muhammadī to express their absolute loyalty to the Prophet as their spiritual and temporal leader.

The Muslim, who recognizes the One God as both Creator and Judge, feels responsible to Him: he believes in His books (the Torah, the Psalms, the Gospels, and the Koran) and in His prophets from Adam through the patriarchs, Moses, and Jesus up to Muhammad, the last lawgiving messenger. Further, he believes in God's angels and in the Last Judgment, and "that good and evil come equally from God." He tries to lead his life according to the revealed law, well aware that God's presence is experienced in every place and every time, and that there is no really profane sphere in life. Fulfillment of cultic duties and the practice of mercy and justice are commanded side by side in the *Koran*: the ritual prayer, ṣalāt, is in almost every instance combined with zakāt, the alms tax. But the worldlings who are embroiled in caring for their wealth, and who neglect religious duties, are threatened by Divine punishment.

Muhammad saw himself at first as a messenger to the Arabs: he was sent to warn them, as no prophet had been sent to them since Abraham. However, only a comparatively small circle of adherents, mainly from the lower classes, gathered around him. The situation did not improve, for the doctrine of the One Supreme God seemed to threaten the main sources of income for the Meccans, i.e., the fairs in honor of various deities and especially the pilgrimage. With the hostility of the Meccans increasing, a group of the new Muslims emigrated to Abyssinia, a Christian country. The situation grew even more difficult after Muhammad, in 619, lost both his wife and his uncle Abu Talib, who, although not converted to Islam, had supported his nephew faithfully. However, new possibilities arose in 621: some inhabitants of Yathrib, north of Mecca, came to perform religious rites and invited Muhammad to join them in their home town, which was torn by internal feuds. After his faithful companions had left Mecca, Muhammad himself, along with his friend Abu Bakr, migrated in June 622 to settle in Yathrib, which soon became known as *madīnat an-nabī*, "the city of the Prophet," or Medina.

The Muslims consider their era to have begun with the date of this emigration (*hijra* or hegira), for at this point a decisive development of Muhammad's activities can be observed: the religious vision of the Meccan revelations had now to be put into communal practice. Furthermore, up to this time the Prophet had considered himself merely as a continuator of the great prophetic religions, Judaism and Christianity. He was convinced that he was preaching the same truth that Jews and Christians had been teaching and practicing. Stories known to us from the Bible can be found in the *Koran*; thus, Sura 12 contains what it calls "the most beautiful story," that of Joseph and his brothers and Potiphar's wife (called Zulaikha in the later tradition), a topic that was to inspire innumerable poets in the Muslim world. However, the Jews refused to accept the revelations connected to their own traditions, for these seemed not to tally completely with the biblical words and to have many gaps. Their objections led Muhammad to the conviction that the Jews had tampered with the revelations in their scripture. He concluded that only the version revealed to him contained the true and real text of these stories and that the faith preached by him on the basis of direct revelation was much older than that professed by the Jews and Christians; his was the pure faith of Abraham who, through Isma'il (Ishmael), is the ancestor of the Arabs and who is said to have founded the central sanctuary in Mecca, the Kaʿba. Pure monotheism, as represented for the first time by Abraham, a *ḥanīf* who had refuted his ancestors' stellar religion, had been corrupted by Jews and Christians and should now become alive again in Islam.

In keeping with this perception of Islam's connection to Abraham, the direction of prayer, till then toward Jerusalem, was changed to Mecca; this made necessary the conquest of Mecca. Eight years after his migration, Muhammad entered his home town in triumph. During these eight years a number of battles were fought: in Badr, 624, a small group of Muslims encountered a strong Meccan army and was victorious, while one year later the Meccans gained a slim victory near Uhud. Three Jewish tribes were overcome and partially uprooted. The Meccans were disquieted by the growing success of their compatriot, but they finally were forced to let him return. He forgave most of those who had worked and plotted against him, but he preferred to stay in Medina. There he eventually died after performing the rites of the pilgrimage in 632. After Khadija's death Muhammad had married several wives (mainly widows); his favorite wife, however, was the young ʿAʾisha, a mere child when he married her. He passed away in her house, and her father Abu Bakr aṣ-Ṣiddīq, "the very faithful one," became his first successor, or "caliph."

The revelations that came upon Muhammad during the last decade of his life are stylistically quite different from the earlier ones: the rhyming prose is less conspicuous and the fiery eschatological threats have given way to discussion of cultic and institutional problems, for Muhammad's role as arbiter and community leader required legal injunctions and rules for the political and social structure of the nascent community. All of life was and is permeated by religion, and just as there is no clear separation between the political and religious aspects of communal life, there are no truly profane acts either. Every act has to begin with the words "in the name of God," *bismillāh*, and must be performed in responsibility to God. The human being stands immediately before God; no mediating priestly caste exists.

IX

IN SEARCH OF MUHAMMAD

WHAT, then, can we conclude about the historicity...of Muhammad's life? Perhaps this that phase one of his life is relatively obscure; phase two, in broad outline, is less obscure; whilst phase three, miracle and misogynist *hadith* aside, is almost wholly authentic. I refer here to the principal events, achievements and speeches rather than to the theological or religious aspects of Muslim conviction about Muhammad. This position is actually remarkably close to that of Sir William Muir... Whilst his estimate of Muhammad's personal conduct was negative and he was critical of much of the material about Muhammad, he yet concluded that the investigator could:

> arrive at a fair approximation to historical fact. Many Gordian knots regarding the prophet of Arabia will remain unsolved, many paradoxes still vainly excite curiosity and baffle explanation. But the groundwork of his career will be laid down with confidence. (1894: lxxvi).

My personal view is that is it comparatively easy to subtract from the collections *hadith* which extol or condemn certain groups or individuals, without compromising the value of much of the legal and historical material, just as the subtraction of many miracle *hadith* leaves the outline of Muhammad's life similarly unimpaired. John Burton (1994) echoes the view of James Robson and other Western writers, that the 'wholesale rejection of the *hadith* as invention and fabrication' cannot be sustained, and that many take us back, if not to the Prophet himself, then to a period 'soon after' (p. 181). In other words, it is possible to recognize bias and fabrication where these exist, but because some of the compilers were arguably dishonest, there is no reason to suppose that they all were. All were human, and as such subject to human faults and failings. I fully accept that fabricated traditions, influenced by bias and party-interest, are to be found in the canonical collections, but nevertheless believe that much of the material is authentic and historically reliable. Although my own view on historicity is thus conservative, I have drawn attention to Crone's and Cook's alternative account.

Whether the mass of *hadith* about how Muhammad ate, washed and treated animals are or are not authentic, is another issue. On the whole, given that the vast bulk of this literature exhorts humane, exemplary behaviour, I am inclined to think that if Muhammad did not say or do what he is reported to have said and done, he indeed might have done! The *hadith*, 'Whatever is in accordance with God's book is from me, whether I really said it or not' may not be far from the mark. In my view, if we extract miracles from Muhammad's biography, including the Night Journey and Ascension, or interpret them metaphorically, and resist attributing to his lips *hadith* which seem to contradict his message (including those which extol or condemn people and places), we are left with a very credible account of a charismatic personality who, as a religious and social reformer, overcame great odds to achieve success and power without ever losing his personal humility and humaneness.

Interestingly, even Muir, who has much to say about the Prophet's moral culpability, includes hardly anything in his extracts from al-Waqidi on Muhammad's 'habits' which does not show Muhammad in a positive light, and this despite his expressed view that 'statements which ... reflect unfavourably on the Prophet' are more likely to be authentic than those which place a halo around him. Similarly, although he also cites *hadith* which, in his view, reflect negatively on Muhammad, Guillaume writes that

> any estimate of his living influence must necessarily be one-sided unless it allows not only for the all-pervading authority and example of the prophet applied to every single detail of human life, but also for the consistent expression of a loving and affectionate concern for mankind. (1924: 99)

In similar vein, he remarks that 'A large section of the *hadith* is full of sayings inculcating the necessity of kindness and love' (*ibid.*: 104), and that

> Trustworthy tradition depicts a man of amazing ability in winning men's hearts by persuasion and in coercing and disarming his opponents. If we ignore the legendary claims to miraculous powers – powers which he himself expressly disclaimed – he stands out as one of the great figures of history ... Far more worthy of credence [than the hagiographical *hadith*] are those stories which go far to explain, when taken with his generosity and kindness, why men such as Umar loved him. (1973: 53–4)

On a personal note, after hours spent reading Bukhari, the picture of Muhammad that stayed in my mind was of a man who was passionate about the welfare of the poor, who disliked ostentation and wealth, and whose often quite simple concept of justice stands the test of time. Thus, 'The rich who do not spend their money on good deeds are in fact the poor' (B 76:13); 'to feed others is a part of Islam' (B 2:6); 'It is illegal for one to sell a thing which has a defect' (B 34:17); 'May Allah's mercy be on him who is lenient in buying, selling and in demanding back his money' (*ibid.*); and 'wish for your brother believer what you like for yourself' (B 2:7) are among the *hadith* which, for me, communicate Muhammad's qualities best of all. Yes, there are *hadith* (on punishment, women, and so on) which I do not find appealing but I actually had a hard job tracing many references to these in other literature to their original source! There are also many *hadith* which remind me of Gospel injunctions, such as B 85:4, 'Allah is more pleased with the repentance of his slave than any one of you is pleased with finding his camel in the desert.'

My object … was to examine the Muhammad of history. However, as I wrote, theological convictions about Muhammad (that *he* was sinless, that his example is 'perfect,' that he enjoyed a 'perfect' or harmonious relationship with the natural world, and so on) constantly mingled with the biographical material, making it all but impossible for me to untangle the two. For example, if we reject the view that he was inspired, then all the efforts devoted to authenticating his *sunnah* by Muslims ever since must be deemed wasted; the Qur'an, and other experiences, such as the *mi'raj*, must presumably be explained away as delusion or wilful contrivance. As noted above, and as I explore more fully later in this book, this is just how non-Muslims have explained away the Muhammad phenomenon. On the other hand, if you believe in Muhammad's inspiration, the evidence becomes self-authenticating; you will accept as authentic both those Qur'anic verses which affirm Muhammad's status and his own claims about that status. Each supports the other, and both support your theological conviction about Muhammad's unique status. This is why Crone calls the Qur'an 'a text without a context' (1995: 269), yet she bases her own arguments on non-Islamic sources. It is, however, because Muslims believe in Muhammad's unique status that they revere him today. Similarly, as stated in the introduction, it is not because he lived in the seventh century and indisputably achieved greatness that they continue to imitate him, but because they believe that he, and no one else, can guide them along God's 'straight path.' As Maududi (1960) says:

> whosoever [would] be a seeker after truth and anxious to become an honest Muslim, a sincere follower of the way of God, it is incumbent upon him to have faith in God's last prophet, accept his teachings, and follow the way he has pointed out to man. This is the real road to success and salvation. (p. 60)

This is why Muhammad exercises what Shabbir Akhtar refers to as 'posthumous authority.' He does not mean, of course, that this authority began after Muhammad's death but that, for Muslims, it remains as important today as it was when he was alive. What I explore ... then, is the even more complex understanding of who Muhammad was which developed from the comparatively simple Qur'anic statements, cited above, that his *sunnah* is the best example,' and his life the last prophetic mission between 632 CE and judgement day. 'To love the Messenger,' says B 3:8, 'is part of faith.' Arguably, as Muslim theology develops a view of Muhammad which goes beyond (some, including Muslims, say far too far beyond) what the Qur'an says about him, the need to possess sources which portray him as exemplary also increases...

Yet is the only option to follow Christ or Muhammad and therefore to choose between the two? Is there any possibility that we are faced not with a choice between rivals but with complementary exemplars, both rooted in divine self-disclosure? If we abandon the idea that either one is inherently better than the other, then I think that we might be able to see Christ and Muhammad as complementary, not as rivals. A difficulty here, as we have already noted, is that Christians and Muslims have both claimed universal recognition for their exemplars. Thus, when I concluded my review of Goddard's book by stating, 'My own view is that such a stark choice may not be necessary. Rather, we may choose to see Muhammad as "supreme exemplar and source of guidance" in some areas of human life, Christ as supreme in others' (Bennett, 1996c: 66–7), I was rebuked by some Christian friends: either I recognize Christ as my absolute Master or I am guilty of compromise. I have thought long and hard about this and disagree. However, I think that my position needs clarification. What I want to argue is that, for me, Christ is indeed supreme exemplar; his love and compassion, his concern for the poor and outcast, his stress on the spirit rather than on the letter of the law, are all absolute values. I do not want to negotiate these. Also, I believe that God was present in the life of Christ in a unique way, conferring a new dignity on human life; I also believe that the qualities and values we see in Christ are those which God wants to govern our conduct. I believe that there is, in Christ, all that is necessary to live according to God's will; nothing more is needed...

What is at issue here is whether only Christians possess genuine knowledge of God, or other religious traditions are also valid paths from which Christians can learn something about their God. Hick sees all religious claims as relative; all represent apprehensions of the ultimately ineffable Real; all are particular because they are mediated by particular historical and cultural contexts...

Hick tends to say that there is no special self-disclosure or revelation; thus we are always dealing with partial, limited human apprehensions. Presumably, however, there is something about the nature of the Real that allows us to glimpse aspects of its nature. Although unknowable in its totality, there is an element of 'knowableness' about the Real. Indeed, Christians, Muslims, Jews and others traditionally go further; they believe that through their prophets and scriptures, God God's-self has taken the initiative. God has revealed to us something about God's nature, qualities, attributes and will.

Unlike Hick, for whom there is no special movement from the divine towards the human, I believe in revelation. Partly, this is based on the fact that human beings have long believed that God makes God's-self known – to Moses at the burning bush, to Job in the whirlwind, through the Christ event, through the scripture revealed to Muhammad. Thus one can either say that this belief is wrong, and that we are always dealing with people who think that God has spoken, or we can say that the Real is by nature a Reality which communicates with humanity. If we claim that our religion enables us to enjoy some sort of relationship with the Ultimate and that this relationship is life-enhancing, we are by definition claiming that the relationship is two-sided. Again, we might simply be wrong. However, those of us who opt for religion, who want to argue that it has some value, do so because we believe that it rests on something other than the human. Yet Hick, I think, is right to call our attention to the human element in religion; without human response, we would also be talking about the overriding of human free will.

Some regard the traditional Islamic view of wahy, in which God's word is communicated through an unconscious Muhammad who 'added nothing to this revelation himself' (Nasr, 1994: 44), as indeed 'overriding human freewill.' Nasr has compared Muhammad's unletteredness with Mary's virginity: the human vehicle of a Divine Message must be pure and untainted ... If this word is in the form of flesh the purity is symbolized by the virginity of the mother ... if it is in the form of a book this purity is symbolized by the unlettered nature of the person who is chosen to announce this word (Ibid.: 44).

However, what I think significant about Muhammad, and Mary, was their willingness to be used by God as God's mediators – in other words, they were receptive to God's revelation. There was, as it were, a meeting between the divine Will and their individual human wills. God wanted to make something of God's-self known; Mary and the Prophet were willing to be used, to place themselves completely in God's hands. Thus, whilst my world-view has a place within it for 'revelation,' I also believe that what God reveals must be humanly encountered. Therefore, whilst Christ and Qur'an/Prophet may be regarded as mirroring the divine (although only as much of the divine as the divine wills to reveal), what we perceive about them will always be tainted by our own agendas and contexts. Unlike Kung, then, I would not insist that Qur'an/Prophet must be regarded as 'God's word attested by the human word,' but I do maintain that our 'reading' of this 'book – prophet text' is a human activity, although one which may be divinely inspired.

If it is possible to claim that our knowledge of God is not merely human apprehension (us talking about God) but God talking about God's-self, or 'God-talk' (albeit this 'God-talk' must be heard through human ears), certain consequences follow; there will be a truthfulness, even an authority, about our apprehending. This is why Christians and Muslims have said: God has spoken, we have heard; his will for us is set forth in Christ or in Qur'an/Muhammad – so, if you want to 'get with the Real' (so to speak) follow us. Newbigin is right to say that if the Christian (and I would add, the Muslim) message is real, 'then to affirm it is no arrogance. To remain quiet about it is treason to our fellow human beings.' The challenge of religious pluralism is this: since we have more than one claim to be 'revelation,' how are we to choose between them? Accept one, reject others? Or, as Hick suggests, regard all as partial? Or, as I am suggesting, regard them as of equal but complementary, rather than rival validity?

In Search of Muhammad

My proposal is rooted in the postmodern view of reality. I accept that we are all captive to our contexts; we all view, indeed construe, reality through the lenses we bring to bear on the data available to us. I am who and what I am – and I need not be anyone else. There is no 'meta-narrative,' there is my narrative and there is yours. Postmodernism has unmasked the element of control behind the meta-narratives we previously took for granted; they are not all to be trusted. They represent the inventions of whatever authority happens to dominate at the time at the centres of power; therefore they can be challenged (for this unmasking, see Foucault, 1977, and the Introduction to this book). This, however, does not mean that we cannot claim that our discourse is worth listening to – but we must relinquish, perhaps, some of the imperialist ways in which we have proclaimed this conviction...

The unanswered question at the heart of the postmodern political agenda is how to make common cause to preserve difference, how to create a sense of solidarity that will be both 'more expansive ... than we presently have' (Rorty, 1989: 196) and conducive to the preservation and enhancement of difference. (Smart, 1993: 105)

Similarly, Akbar Ahmed (1992: 27) writes about the 'positive and exhilarating offering, what Barthes calls "jouissance,"' which 'postmodernism brings to us: the importance of diversity, the need for tolerance, the necessity for understanding the other')... Thus, in the postmodern world, we can claim to have a message of universal significance but must renounce the type of 'universalism' that seeks to 'impose' this on others. Christian and Muslim evangelism have both, at times, enjoyed an alliance with political and economic structures which has left people with little real 'religious freedom'; they have found conversion the most pragmatic option. Postmodernity invites us to win the intellectual debate – and to re-examine how we may have converted people in bygone days...

What I want to argue, then, is this: Christ, for me, will be the mirror which I shall hold up before any claim to reflect the will of God. In applying this measure, I am not claiming superiority; my only claim is that I have something that works for me, which enables me to make sense of the world. It is my hermeneutical framework. However, not everything which claims to be of God, inside the Christian religion as well as outside it, will match the image in my mirror. Sometimes, beliefs or practices will strike discord. Christ condemned that which enslaves or manipulates people; he spoke out against oppression. He affirmed the dignity and worth of all. He rejected the accumulation of wealth – he encourages us to store up treasure which endures eternally. Thus systems which privilege some over others, which elevate profit above people, will find no reflection in my mirror. I will need to reflect, 'Have I seen aright?' before I speak, lest I be guilty of misconstruing what I see. However, I believe that the Gospel does compel me to oppose the forces of darkness. There are moral principles which inform my world-view and I will not yield ground when these principles are threatened. I will always remain open to dialogue. I will listen to my enemies. However, if their arguments do not convince me, I will do all I can to persuade others that my view, not theirs, is right. 'Enemies,' of course, is a strong term; yet those who value success, wealth, possessions, over against fairness, compassion, justice, may well qualify as such. So might those who think that some ethnicities are inherently better than others! In other words, whilst I do not want to privilege my way of seeing the world over-and-above other peoples,' I also uphold my right to argue for what I believe is just and right. I agree with Kung (see below) and Halliday that the goal may be to achieve a consensus on core values. I am not yet willing to concede that no moral principles can be regarded as absolute. Halliday (1996: 154) writes:

> we are to some degree in a common ethical universe in which an absolute 'cultural relativist' position is untenable … If, as is often argued, attempts to produce moral codes on the basis of an irreducible, internationally recognized minimum have not yet succeeded, this does not gainsay the principle that some such elements are to be acknowledged.

What can I say of Muhammad, when thus addressed? Here, I follow Kung's view that, for me as a Christian, Muhammad can serve as a 'prophetic corrective' – summoning me to re-examine what stands at the centre of my life, reminding me that there must be symmetry between what I say and what I do: 'That faith and life, orthodoxy and orthopraxy, belong together everywhere, including politics' (1984: 129). Jomier (1989) suggests that Christians might regard Muhammad as a 'charismatic reformer'; Jomier's book *How to Understand Islam*, with a chapter on 'The Problem of Muhammad,' enjoys the nihil obstat and imprimatur of a Catholic bishop. Jomier is a Dominican priest and missionary. Muslims, though, may think that this view of Muhammad falls short of what the *shahadah* demands – belief in his messengership, 'And Muhammad is the messenger of God.' Incidentally, I do not know how the Qur'an was communicated by God through Muhammad, but I can accept that it was; as I view the incarnation as a mystery, so I view the *bookilication* of the Qur'an.

As I look at the life of Muhammad, I see a life which, although Christians have contrasted it negatively with Christ's, can be interpreted as complementary; Christ said 'Render to Caesar' but did not give us instructions on how Caesar ought to spend the tax to which he is entitled. Muhammad's *sunnah* can help to supply some detail here; see Zakaria (1988: 36–7) on 'the rate of taxation and the mode of collection ... determined by the Prophet.' Christ appears to have been a pacifist. This may indeed be the Christian ideal. However, in practice, Christians have had to develop theories to justify war in certain mitigating circumstances; Phipps (1996: 156) comments that 'Christian rulers from Constantine onwards have been as interested in legitimizing war as in making peace.' Muhammad's use of war, thus interpreted, does not contradict Christian practice. Indeed, as Esack (1996) says, Muhammad was given 'permission for the armed struggle' in order to help preserve the sanctity of Christian and Jewish, as well as Muslim, institutions; 'But for the fact that God continues to repel some people by means of others, churches, synagogues and mosques, [all places] wherein God's name is mentioned, would be razed to the ground' (p. 161; Q 22:40).

F. D. Maurice (1805–72) addressed the relationship between Christianity and other faiths in his classic *The Religions of the World* (1846) and, anticipating Kung by almost 140 years, spoke about 'The Mahometan side of Christianity,' and about Muhammad as 'one of God's witnesses before the Cross' (p. 238). Muhammad's insistence that 'God is' and is 'the ground of action, history and knowledge' challenges a Christianity which has too often tried to substitute 'notions and theories about [God's] nature' for the simple, uncompromising message that it is God who 'is himself the ground of man's being' (p. 33; note this pioneer use of the expression 'ground of being' usually associated with Paul Tillich).. On the other hand, and I am personally inclined towards a pacifist stance, it can be argued that the rules governing war which have been handed down from the Prophet, through Abu Bakr especially, are such that no modern war could meet them. These protect non-combatants, crops, houses, places of worship; prisoners of war must be properly fed and clothed, although they may be ransomed. I recently heard a Muslim colleague endorse this view.

My own perception (drawing on Maurice) is that Islam has veered towards over-emphasis on the letter of the law, whilst (as Nasr has pointed out) Christianity has been too 'esoteric.' What is needed is a meeting of the ways; Christ may challenge Muslims to re-examine the ethical intent of the Qur'an, to pursue the Qur'anic spirit rather than the Qur'anic 'letter.' Christ, as 'a Spirit from God' (Q 4:171) may be a *sunnah* here for Muslims. Christianity may have neglected justice in the here and now in favour of reward tomorrow, and has rightly attracted Marxist critique. As Harvey Cox (1988) points out, religious institutions have often 'played an almost exclusively reactionary role. Marx and his followers took deadly [but accurate] aim ... controlled by the dominant groups, religion can be a tool of manipulation' (p. 214). Here, Muhammad's *sunnah*, with its many safeguards against the misuse of power (even if these have not always been practised by his successors) may serve as a 'prophetic corrective' for Christians.

For Muhammad's 'preferential option for the *mustad'afun'* (oppressed of the earth, marginalized) see Esack, 1997: 100–1:

> to facilitate the empowerment of the poor and dispossessed, the qur'an announces that in the wealth of the rich there is an intrinsic share for them (70:25; 51:19). The principle of distributive justice was unambiguously affirmed ... elaborating on this principle, the Prophet mentioned various forms of wealth and power that had to be shared with those who did not have them. (p. 101)

We know that Muhammad had to be persuaded to take enough from the *Bait-al-Mal* to provide for himself and his family, and that at the height of his success he chose to live quite frugally (see Muir, 1894: 515–16). Phipps (1996) has a useful discussion of 'Getting and Giving' in Islam and Christianity (pp. 127–34), 'Giving to the needy should be viewed as a dividing of wealth that does not ultimately belong to the human giver' (p. 128). The preacher in me says, 'Surely here is a *sunnah* for me, as a Christian, which complements Christ's concern for the poor and marginalized who, he said, "would inherit the Kingdom."'

...I am not persuaded that attributing validity to aspects of Muhammad's *sunnah* (example) reduces Christ to anything less than Christians have traditionally believed him to be – God made human, in whom the fullness of God's will for human life was revealed. To say that aspects of Muhammad's *sunnah* have a validity for me which equals Christ's teaching is to say no more than that these aspects are wholly consistent with what I know of God in Christ; they do not *contradict*, but are *consonant with*, that revelation. This does not mean that God cannot use other channels to flesh out the details of the life he wants us to live. Saying that God speaks to us through other religions is not the same as saying that he 'saves' through them. God will, I am convinced, save whom he wills to save...

My research suggests that what we bring to the historical record determines, to a large extent, what we take away, how we see Muhammad. There may be as many images of Muhammad as there are readers of this book. None the less, I hope that something of Muhammad's undeniable genius, perhaps even of his 'excellence,' might be found reflected in my research (Phil, 1: 9–11). For me, Muhammad's *sunnah* contains much that is worth putting into practice.

X

THE PROPHET MUHAMMAD:
A BIOGRAPHY

THE life of the Prophet Muhammad is a story of overpowering pathos and beauty. It is history, tragedy and enlightenment compressed into one tale. It is also a story virtually unknown to the West... Within Islam, however, he represents almost everything of human value. Muhammad, Prophet of God, the last and greatest of that long line of men, from Adam through to Abraham, Moses and Jesus, who have struggled to bring the world of God to mankind. Even when viewed in an entirely secular perspective he remains a superhero. He was founder of the Caliphate, one of the greatest empires of the world; creator of classical Arabic, a new literature and world language; founder of a new national identity, the Arab; and creator of Islam, a worldwide culture that is now 1,200 million strong and growing more rapidly than you can count. Only by marrying the best qualities of certain characters from European civilisation – a combination, say, of Alexander the Great, Diogenes and Aristotle, or the Emperor Constantine, St Paul and St Francis – can you begin to understand the measure of the man.

Of course, his historical achievements were mere accidental spin-offs. His only purpose was to forge a new relationship between God and mankind. To those billions of believers who follow in his spiritual path he is omnipresent within the individual world of imagination, prayer and petition. He is perceived in many ways. He is the ultimate stern patriarch, that man of men who stands at the forefront of all the saints, heroes and good rulers from centuries of proud Muslim history. He is the implacable lawgiver, the guide who has clearly pointed out the roads of destiny: this way leads to heaven, this way to hell. He is the loving grandfather, leading the prayers in the mosque while his infant grandson clambers upon his shoulders. He is the sacrificial hero who goes into the testing fire of the spiritual world for the benefit of mankind, shaken to the core of his very being by the terror of being addressed by God through the angels – and all the while persecuted and reviled by his own people. He is the great lover of women – he required no other luxuries, no possessions, so complete was his joy and satisfaction in the company of his wives. He is the wise sage who despised the luxurious trappings of royalty, the halls, guards, courtiers, silks and gold that hitherto had always been associated with power. He is also the savant of the mystics, the guide who has led generations of dervishes, sufis, poets and lovers of God on their quests. He is the only man to have journeyed to heaven and back. He is the Hero of Heroes…

As the sun rises over each successive longitude of the globe, the dawn prayer ripples out from the throats of the faithful, so that the whole world is now encircled in a continuous wave of praise. Muhammad's greatest gift to the world is revealed every time a Muslim stands alone to pray directly to God. This revolution in spiritual attitude, the direct communion between believer and deity, is Muhammad's triumphant achievement. He himself always possessed an extraordinarily close relationship with the divine, revealed in that haunting revelation that 'God is closer to you than your jugular vein.' This intimacy had its own personal price, for he was overwhelmed by the sense of the omnipotence of the deity and the insignificance of mankind, leading to a fear that the end of the world was but a breath away. This heavy sense of foreboding helps explain the decisiveness with which he acted in the last years of his life.

Muhammad was enormously proud to stand in a line of succession with the prophets of old. Islam freely drew from the great reservoir of religious experience: the ethical teachings of Christ were combined with the family and community centred religious life of the Jews. An intellectually elegant and conceptually sturdy monotheism was combined with a passionate awareness of a Day of Judgement. But Muhammad was also the Prophet of the Arabs. His Islam quarried the noble traditions of the Arabs. It took the loyalty and strong sense of community that had been hitherto focused on the clan and tribe, and extended it to embrace the whole society of believers. It extracted the virtues of the Bedouin: their exquisite sense of hospitality, their generosity and their reckless chivalry, but rejected their intemperance, casual cruelty and ignorance. It elevated the fine qualities of the successful caravan merchants (their hilm – self-control – and aql – rational judgement) but directed it away from personal ambition to the communal care of the weak and the poor. Islam suppressed the blood feud and replaced it with a community that collectively enforced public justice, defended itself and took responsibility for education and social welfare. The old traditions of tribal raiding were replaced by the jihad, the struggle against the unbelievers on the frontiers of Islam and in the hearts of the hypocrites.

A Muslim must believe that the Qur'an comes from God. Muhammad's role was to shape this divine inspiration into a language that could not only be understood but could inspire his fellow Arabs. This was his genius; to transform his own religious experience, which was by its very nature highly individual, and create from it something of relevance to a whole society and indeed to succeeding generations. There is an unearthly, timeless magic about the Qur'an. There are verses in it that must have seemed mysterious and indecipherable for centuries, but which suddenly glow with an acute relevance in later ages whose outlook has been changed by scientific discoveries and an expanding understanding of the world. In the farewell sermon, the Prophet had declared to his people, 'I leave behind me two things, the Qur'an and my example, the Sunnah, and if you follow these you will never go astray.'

It has been a challenge that many societies have grappled with but very few have managed to meet. Within Islam all that is of merit in mankind is embodied by the Prophet Muhammad. As Rumi, the great mystic medieval poet, declared, 'He is the evidence of God's existence,' while Muhammad said of himself, 'I, too, am a man like you.'

Peace be upon you, Prophet of God.

XI

MUHAMMAD, PROPHET FOR OUR TIME

THE Qur'an is the holy word of God, and its authority remains absolute. But Muslims know that it is not always easy to interpret. Its laws were designed for a small community, but a century after their Prophet's death, Muslims ruled a vast empire, stretching from the Himalayas to the Pyrenees. Their circumstances were entirely different from those of the Prophet and the first Muslims, and Islam had to change and adapt. The first essays in Muslim history were written to address current perplexities. How could Muslims apply the Prophet's insights and practice to their own times? When the early biographers told the story of his life, they tried to explain some of the passages in the Qur'an by reproducing the historical context in which these particular revelations had come down to Muhammad. By understanding what had prompted a particular Qur'anic teaching, they could relate it to their own situation by means of a disciplined process of analogy. The historians and thinkers of the time believed that learning about the Prophet's struggles to make the word of God audible in the seventh century would help them to preserve his spirit in their own. From the very start, writing about the Prophet Muhammad was never a wholly antiquarian pursuit. The process continues today. Some Muslim fundamentalists have based their militant ideology on the life of Muhammad; Muslim extremists believe that he would have condoned and admired their atrocities. Other Muslims are appalled by these claims, and point to the extraordinary pluralism of the Qur'an, which condemns aggression and sees all rightly guided religions as deriving from the one God. We have a long history of Islamophobia in Western culture that dates back to the time of the Crusades. In the twelfth century, Christian monks in Europe insisted that Islam was a violent religion of the sword, and that Muhammad was a charlatan who imposed his religion on a reluctant world by force of arms; they called him a lecher and a sexual pervert. This distorted version of the Prophet's life became one of the received ideas of the West, and Western people have always found it difficult to see Muhammad in a more objective light. Since the destruction of the World Trade Center on September II, 2001, members of the Christian Right in the United States and some sectors of the Western media have continued this tradition of hostility, claiming that Muhammad was irredeemably addicted to war. Some have gone so far as to claim that he was a terrorist and a pedophile.

We can no longer afford to indulge this type of bigotry, because it is a gift to extremists who can use such statements to "prove" that the Western world is indeed engaged on a new crusade against the Islamic world. Muhammad was not a man of violence. We must approach his life in a balanced way, in order to appreciate his considerable achievements. To cultivate an inaccurate prejudice damages the tolerance, liberality, and compassion that are supposed to characterize Western culture.

I became convinced of this fifteen years ago, after the fatwah of Ayatollah Khomeini had sentenced Salman Rushdie and his publishers to death because of what was perceived to be a blasphemous portrait of Muhammad in *The Satanic Verses*. I abhorred the fatwah and believed that Rushdie had a right to publish whatever he chose, but I was disturbed by the way some of Rushdie's liberal supporters segued from a denunciation of the fatwah to an out-and-out condemnation of Islam itself that bore no relation to the facts. It seemed wrong to defend a liberal principle by reviving a medieval prejudice. We appeared to have learned nothing from the tragedy of the 1930s, when this type of bigotry made it possible for Hitler to kill six million Jews. But I realized that many Western people had no opportunity to revise their impression of Muhammad, so I decided to write a popular accessible account of his life to challenge this entrenched image. The result was *Muhammad: A Biography of the Prophet*, which was first published in 1991. But in the wake of September 11, we need to focus on other aspects of Muhammad's life. So this is a completely new and entirely different book, which, I hope, will speak more directly to the terrifying realities of our post–September 11 world.

As a paradigmatic personality, Muhammad has important lessons, not only for Muslims, but also for Western people. His life was jihad: as we shall see, this word does not mean "holy war," it means "struggle." Muhammad literally sweated with the effort to bring peace to war-torn Arabia, and we need people who are prepared to do this today. His life was a tireless campaign against greed, injustice, and arrogance. He realized that Arabia was at a turning point in that the old way of thinking would no longer suffice, so he wore himself out in the creative effort to evolve an entirely new solution. We entered another era of history on September 11, and must strive with equal intensity to develop a different outlook.

Strangely, events that took place in seventh-century Arabia have much to teach us about the events of our time and their underlying significance – far more, in fact, than the facile sound bites of politicians. Muhammad was not trying to impose religious orthodoxy and was not much interested in metaphysics – but to change people's hearts and minds. He called the prevailing spirit of his time *jahiliyyah*. Muslims usually understand this to mean the "Time of Ignorance," that is, the pre-Islamic period in Arabia. But, a recent research shows, Muhammad used the term *jahiliyyah* to refer not to an historical era but to a state of mind that caused violence and terror in seventh-century Arabia. *Jahiliyyah*, I would argue, is also much in evidence in the West today as well as in the Muslim world.

Paradoxically, Muhammad became a timeless personality because he was so rooted in his own period. We cannot understand his achievement unless we appreciate what he was up against. In order to see what he can contribute to our own predicament, we must enter the tragic world that made him a prophet nearly fourteen hundred years ago, on a lonely mountain top just outside the holy city of Mecca.

The Birth of the Prophet

INTRODUCTION

BAYARD Taylor is best seen as part of a tradition which extends from
the late eighteenth century through the nineteenth to the present –
mainly the American search for an identity and role in the modern
world. Interest in the outside world was a prominent feature of
nineteenth-century America, and the Americans were proving that
they could not in the long run be as inward-looking as the momentous
rise in the spirit of nationalism, especially after the second war with
Britain, had tended to make them. Nineteenth-century Americans
traveled extensively; first to Europe, then to the Near East, North
Africa, Persia, and the Indian subcontinent, and later to the Far East.
Books of travel surged in popularity, and translations of Near Eastern
material, in addition to original works, appeared in a large number of
magazines and journals. As a result, traditional European misconceptions about the Arab-Islamic world gradually gave way to a less biased
attitude. This growing interest was shared by architects and furniture
designers, merchants and missionaries, politicians and poets. Bayard
Taylor, who visited the area three times during the course of his life,
must be considered a key figure in this movement. The Near East
figures prominently not only in his *Poems of the Orient* (1854), which
represents a peak in his Eastern interest, but in various other works. The
collection, however, was the first of its kind in American literature.

93

The Birth of the Prophet

Poets, one must assume, are never secluded from the political, social and cultural concerns of their nations. This is particularly applicable in the case of Taylor, who was not only an artist and a man of letters, but also (and concurrently) a diplomat and representative of the 'American way.' His role as translator was most poignant in this regard as he in effect was constructing a bridge across cultures. In his movement towards the Near East, Taylor was an heir to a spirit of pioneering and more immediately in his time to the Romantic tradition, which had had its roots in the European experience and consciousness. Taylor's contribution to the American interest in the Near East, especially to the genre of the Near Eastern poem in nineteenth-century American literature, was both considerable and worthwhile – his *Poems of the Orient* (in addition to other long individual poems) devoted its entire length to Near Eastern themes. It is significant that William Alger, Thomas Aldrich, and Richard Stoddard published their Eastern collections after the publication of *Poems of the Orient*.

There is no doubt that Taylor's popularity as a poet or the particular appeal of his Near Eastern poetry drew strength from his several roles in public life as a man of action, journalist, diplomat, traveler, and lecturer. His travel accounts, which were being published as he was still touring the Near East and Africa, made a strong impact at home. The exaggerated accounts and news in the media of his intentions to drive through undiscovered regions made the public await his correspondence in the *Tribune* with much eagerness and anticipation. And as masses of Americans increasingly turned to newspapers and magazines for more easily available and interesting material than books, the impact of such accounts and news was widespread. His lectures, his several pictures and portraits in Near Eastern costume, and his songs excited great interest and attention, thus creating a legend, and turning Taylor into 'a cultural phenomena of considerable interest and popularity.' He was read and admired by the ordinary man in America as well as by the major *Literati* in both Europe and America. Again it may be significant that Taylor who developed these several roles very successfully in the Near East had done so via Europe.

Certainly Taylor is sincere in his attempt to redress the Arab-Islamic image in the West. He accuses the majority of Western travelers of misrepresentation and describes them as 'the ignorant,' 'the complainer,' 'the desponder,' and 'the depreciating,' while presenting himself indirectly as 'the sympathetic' traveler, one who endeavours to transcend the narrow boundaries of sect and creed in a perception of universal truth. Taylor is at pains to convince his audience as much as himself that he was not an imposter but, rather, 'an humble follower in the steps of Burkhardt and Layard.'

He states further in an unpublished lecture entitled 'The Arabs':

> No travellers, except the lamented Burkhardt and Layard, the Ninevite, have done justice to the nobler qualities which so eminently characterizes the Arab race. These travellers claim our confidence, for they speak as those having authority. They pursued the only true method of travel, by adopting, as far as possible, the habits of the people with whom they were thrown, – wearing their dress, speaking their languages, and respecting the faith and traditions which they held sacred.

Much ahead of his time, Taylor, most poignantly expresses his resentment for the largely unstudied and destructive excavations carried out by some Western archaeologists and contractors who were motivated by financial greed and little concern for scientific knowledge – people Taylor described as 'carrying a mallet and chisel and leaving records of their "vulgar vanity".'

Although he accused other travellers of misrepresentation, he himself, fell, on some occasions into the same trap. Indeed, even with the best intentions, it is not easy to understand the complexities of any culture or people in a relatively short period of time. Taylor, like many other travellers, failed to realize that to understand and represent the Eastern cultures to the Western mind was a task which required a lot more than months of travel or the knowledge of a few words or phrases, or alternatively, the indulgence in certain habits or activities.

The Near East does not figure strongly or prominently in Taylor's other poetical works though images and metaphors of isolated and fragmentary nature appear infrequently here and there. Perhaps Taylor was able to control his Eastern streak and compartmentalize it separately from his other activities, but, seen in perspective, he lacked the ability and the genius to completely master his various social roles and other manifestations of his energy. He once wrote to a friend: "How should I dare think of poetry, when there is a murder trial, two accidents, and a religious anniversary to put in shape for the evening paper!" This, perhaps, was one of the reasons why he failed to become – as he always desperately desired – a 'great poet' with everlasting fame and appeal.

Taylor, though reflecting in many ways the concerns of his age, did not indulge in the spiritualism or transcendentalism pursued by many of his contemporary poets and friends. One must remember that he was following in the tradition of Browning, whose scepticism of spiritualism and of its professional advocates – influencing Taylor's own contempt of charlatans who were trying to exploit the age's desperate interest in spiritual matters in the face of the growing materialism and industrialism. It is a credit to Taylor that he did not exaggerate the 'mystical' quality of the East as he might have been expected to do. His travels in that part of the world exposed him to realities which counter balanced the fictitious image of the East in Western mind. He himself once commented: 'I am more interested in a live Arab, than a dead Pharaoh.'

The interest in Taylor, especially immediately after his death in 1878, inevitably dwindled with the shift, on a national level, from a global awareness, in which the Near East figures prominently, to a more domestic emphasis. However, through articles, travel books, lectures, poetry, portraits in Near Eastern costume, and the widely popular 'Bedouin Song' which was set to music, and was still being sung in the 1920's, Taylor helped more than any other nineteenth-century American to perpetuate the lure of the Near East (and to certain extent the Far East). Because of such popularity his impact and influence were far reaching in bringing the Arab-Islamic Near East within the reach of a wide section of the American public. His often unconventional approach to the Arabs and Islam, as well as the injection of his material with new significance through his tolerance, sensitivity, and humanistic views, helped him lead a new approach developed by Gibbon, Goethe, and Carlyle in Europe, and Irving in America.

In spite of Taylor's influence, the Near East was a passing vogue which never took lasting roots in American literature, but it certainly helped to enrich and diversify it. Nevertheless, one cannot dismiss the closeness of that experience to the American psyche since certain important features of that experience survived and surfaced during several later episodes in American history. Thus the approach to the Near East, historically early and formative to both politicians and poets in America, was later adopted in confrontations, or at least encounters, between the American nation and other foreign states and cultures. One may assume therefore that the contact with the Near East helped to establish a pattern in American politics and letters. However, issues which were nearer to the domestic scene and more deeply entrenched in the American (and largely Western) ethos were bound to be still more fervently and far more convincingly presented. Such works are inevitably closer to home and, if handled by writers or poets of superior talents, are destined to have longer life and a more enduring quality and appeal.

What may be considered to be one of Taylor's most impressive works in changing attitudes towards the Arab-Islamic world was 'The Birth of the Prophet' in his 1854 collection *Poems of the Orient*. This poem, with reverence and sensitivity, honors the prophet Muhammad, who brought the universal message of Islam to mankind – spreading from the cradle of Arabia to the far corners of the Earth.

Taken, and adapted from the unpublished 'Bayard Taylor and his Contemporaries: The Near East in Nineteenth-Century American Poetry' by Anas S. Al-Shaikh-Ali, PhD Thesis, Victoria University of Manchester, UK, 1983.

THE BIRTH OF THE PROPHET

I.

THRICE three moons had waxed in heaven, thrice three moons had
waned away,
Since Abdullah, faint and thirsty, on the Desert's bosom lay
In the fiery lap of Summer, the meridian of the day;

II.

SINCE from out the sand upgushing, lo! a sudden fountain leapt;
Sweet as musk and clear as amber, to his parching lips it crept.
When he drank it straightway vanished, but his blood its virtue kept.

III.

ERE the morn his forehead's lustre, signet of the Prophet's line,
To the beauty of Amina had transferred its flame divine:
Of the germ within her sleeping, such the consecrated sign.

IV.

AND with every moon that faded waxed the splendor more and more,
Till Amina's beauty lightened through the matron veil she wore,
And the tent was filled with glory, and of Heaven it seemed the door.

V.

WHEN her quickened womb its burden had matured, and Life began
Struggling in its living prison, through the wide Creation ran
Premonitions of the coming of a God-appointed man.

The Birth of the Prophet

VI.

FOR the oracles of Nature recognize a Prophet's birth
Blossom of the tardy ages, crowning type of human worth
And by miracles and wonders he is welcomed to the Earth.

VII.

THEN the stars in heaven grew brighter, stooping down ward from their zones;
Wheeling round the towers of Mecca, sang the moon in silver tones,
And the Kaaba's grisly idols trembled on their granite thrones.

VIII.

MIGHTY arcs of rainbow splendor, pillared shafts of purple fire,
Split the sky and spanned the darkness, and with many a golden spire,
Beacon-like, from all the mountains streamed the lambent meteors higher.

IX.

BUT when first the breath of being to the sacred infant came,
Paled the pomp of airy lustre, and the stars grew dim with shame,
For the glory of his countenance outshone their feebler flame.

X.

OVER Nedjid's sands it lightened, unto Oman's coral deep,
Startling all the gorgeous regions of the Orient from sleep,
Till, a sun on night new-risen, it illumed the Indian steep.

XI.

THEY who dwelt in Mecca's borders saw the distant realms appear
All around the vast horizon, shining marvellous and clear,
From the gardens of Damascus unto those of Bendomeer.

The Birth of the Prophet

XII.

FROM the colonnades of Tadmor to the hills of Hadramaut,
Ancient Araby was lighted, and her sands the splendor caught,
Till the magic sweep of vision overtook the track of Thought.

XIII.

SUCH on Earth the wondrous glory, but beyond the sevenfold skies
God His mansions filled with gladness, and the seraphs saw arise
Palaces of pearl and ruby from the founts of Paradise.

XIV.

AS the surge of heavenly anthems shook the solemn midnight air,
From the shrines of false religions came a wailing of despair,
And the fires on Pagan altars were extinguished every where.

XV.

MID the sounds of salutation, mid the splendor and the balm,
Knelt the sacred child, proclaiming, with a brow of heavenly calm:
"God is God; there is none other; I his chosen Prophet am!"

Bayard Taylor
As published in his *Poems of the Orient* (1854)

Notes

Preface

1. Hans Koechler, "Religion, Reason and Violence: Pope Benedict XVI and Islam",
    Statement by the President of the International Progress Organization, Prof. Dr. Hans
    Koechler, on the lecture delivered by Pope Benedict XVI at the University of
    Regensburg on 12 September 2006, Vienna, 16 September 2006, P/RE/19920, (at:
    http://i-p-o.org/koechler-Religion_Reason_Violence-16Sept06.htm), accessed:
    February 12, 2009).

2. Maxime Rodinson, *Muhammad: Prophet of Islam*, London: Tauris Parke Paperbacks,
    2002, pp. 76–82.

3. Zafar Ali Qureshi, *Prophet Muhammad and His Western Critic: A Critique of W.
    Montgomery Watt and Others*, Lahore: Idara Ma'arif Islami, 1992, p. 1.

Introduction

1. Minou Reeves, *Muhammad in Europe*, Reading: Garnet, 2000, p. 1; cf. Clinton
    Bennett, *In Search of Muhammad*, London: Cassell, 1998, pp. 69–92.

2. Richard Fletcher, *The Cross and the Crescent, Christianity and Islam from Muhammad to
    the Reformation*, London: Allen Lane, 2003, p. 10.

3. Qureshi, *Prophet Muhammad and His Western Critics*, pp. 1–12.

4. Reeves, *Muhammad in Europe*, p. 2.

5. Reeves, *Muhammad in Europe*, p. 3.

6. Fletcher, *The Cross and the Crescent*, pp. 16–17.

7. Philip Almond, "Western Images of Islam, 1700–1900," The Australian Journal of
    Politics and History 49.3 (2003).

8. Reeves, *Muhammad in Europe*, pp. 73–74. Cf. Tomaž Mastnak, *Islam and the Creation of*

Notes

European Identity, CSD Perspectives, London: Centre for the Study of Democracy, 1994.

9. Bennett, *In Search of Muhammad*, p. 89; Tomaž Mastnak, *Crusading Peace: Christendom, the Muslim World, and Western Political Order*, Berkeley: University of California Press, 2002, pp. 168–172. Mastnak seriously questions Peter's idealised image as a "pacifist", though.

10. Reeves, *Muhammad in Europe*, pp. 90–92.

11. Bennett, *In Search of Muhammad*, p. 88.

12. Mastnak, *Crusading Peace*, pp. 196–97.

13. Reeves, *Muhammad in Europe*, pp. 109–111.

14. Almond, "Western Images of Islam."

15. See R. A. Davenport's introduction to the 1891 edition of Sale's work.

16. Almond, "Western Images of Islam."

17. Henri Boulainvilliers *The Life of Mohammad (or the Life of Mahomet)*, Piscataway, NJ: Gorgias Press, 2002, p. 244.

18. Matthew Birchwood, 'Vindicating The Prophet,' *Prose Studies*, 29:1, (2007), p. 64.

19. Birchwood, 'Vindicating The Prophet,' pp. 64–66.

20. Reeves, *Muhammad in Europe*, pp. 73–118.

21. Almond, "Western Images of Islam."

22. Reeves, *Muhammad in Europe*, p. 171.

23. Mastnak, *"Islam and Europe,"* p. 39.

24. Reeves, *Muhammad in Europe*, p. 180.

25. Almond, "Western Images of Islam."

26. Almond, "Western Images of Islam."

27. Almond, "Western Images of Islam."

28. Edward W Said, *Orientalism*, London: Routledge, 1978.

29. Mastnak, "Islam and Europe," p. 39.

30. Edmund Burke III, "Orientalism and World History: Representing Middle Eastern Nationalism and Islamism in the Twentieth Century," *Theory & Society*, 27:4 (August 1998), 589–607 (p. 490).

31. Ziauddin Sardar, *Orientalism*, Buckingham: Open University Press, 1999, p. 78.

32. Elie Kedourie, *Democracy and Arab Political Culture*, London: Routledge, p. 1.

33. Burke III, "Orientalism and World History", p. 504.

34. Sardar, *Orientalism*, pp. 81–2.

35. Sardar, *Orientalism*, pp. 85–92.

36. Bernard Lewis, *What Went Wrong? Western Impact and Middle East Responses* (Oxford University Press, 2002).

37. Kramer, Martin (ed) (1997) *The Islamism Debate*, Tel Aviv: The Moshe Dayan Centre, p. 171.

Notes

Chapter VI

1. Ibn Hisham, pp. 217–20; cf. Ibn Sa'd, vol. I, pt. 1, pp. 136–9.
2. D. G. Hogarth, *Arabia* (Oxford, 1922) p. 52.
3. Koran 5: 92. The Nabateans had anti-bacchic deity.
4. Cf. Koran 2: 168.
5. Fasting was ordained in the Medinese period, long after the Abyssinian migration; Koran, 2 : 179, 183. Ibn Hisham, p. 219.

Chapter VII

1. *The Life of Muhammad*, A. Guillaume, trans. (London: Oxford University Press, 1955) p. 107.
2. Ibn Hisham, as quoted in Phillip K. Hitti, *History of the Arabs*, 9th ed. (New York: St. Martin's Press, 1966) p. 120.
3. Samuel 17: 45, *The Oxford Annotated Bible: Revised Standard Version* (New York: Oxford University Press, 1962). See also Exodus 14: 14, Deutronomy 20: 41, 1 Samuel 15: 33, 1 Kings 18: 36–40, and 2 Kings 10: 25–31.
4. Geoffrey Parinder, *Mysticism in the World's Religions* (New York: Oxford University Press, 1976) p. 121.

Chapter IX

Ahmed, Akbar (1992) *Postmodernism and Islam: Predicament and Promise*, London, BBC Books.

Bennett, Clinton (1996c) 'Review of Hugh Goddard's *Christians and Muslims*', *Discernment: An Ecumenical Journal of Inter-religious Encounter* NS 2:3 and 3:1, pp. 64.7.

Burton, John (1994) *An Introduction to the Hadith*, Edinburgh, Edinburgh University Press.

Cox, Harvey (1988) *Many Mansions: A Christian's Encounter with Other Faiths*, London, Collins.

Crone, Patricia (1995) 'Review of F. E. Peter's *Muhammad and the Origins of Islam*', *Journal of the Royal Asiatic Society*, 3rd Series, 5:2, pp. 269–72.

Esack, Farid (1997) *Qur'an, Liberation and Pluralism*, Oxford, Oneworld.

Foucault, Michel (1977) *Discipline and Punish: The Birth of the Prison*, London, Allen Lane.

Guillaume, Alfred (1924) *The Traditions of Islam*, Oxford, Oxford University Press.

Guillaume, Alfred (1973) *Islam*, Harmondsworth, Penguin. Originally published in 1954.

Halliday, Fred (1996) *Islam and the Myth of Confrontation. Religion and Politics in the Middle East*, London, I. B. Tauris.

Jomier, Jaques (1989) *How to Understand Islam*, London, SCM Press.

Küng, Hans (1984) *Christianity and the World Religions*, London, SCM Press.

Maududi, Abul Ala (1960) *Towards Understanding Islam*, London, UK Islamic Mission.

Notes

Maurice, Frederick Denison (1846) *The Religions of the World*, London, Macmillan.

Muir, William (1894) *Life of Mahomet*, third (abridged) edition, London, Smith, Elder and Co. Originally published in 4 vols in 1857–61.

Nasr, Seyyed Hossein (1994) Ideas and Realities of Islam, revised edition, London, The Aqurian Press. Originally published in 1966.

Phipps, William E. (1996) *Muhammad and Jesus: A Comparison of the Prophets and Their Teaching*, London, SCM.

Rorty, Richard (1989) *Contingency, Irony and Solidarity*, Cambridge, Cambridge University Press.

Smart, Barry (1993) *Postmodernity*, London, Routledge.

Zakaria, Rafiq (1988) *The Struggle Within Islam: The Conflict Between Religion and Politics*, Harmondsworth, Penguin.

Sources

Chapter I:

Taken from *The Koran: Commonly Called The Alkoran of Mohammed* by George Sale, pp. iii–vi. Originally published by J. Wilcox, London, UK, 1734.

Chapter II:

Taken from *The Hero as Prophet. Mahomet: Islam* (Lecture II, 8th May 1840), in *On Heroes, Hero-Worship and the Heroic in History* by Thomas Carlyle, pp. 38–69. Originally published by Frederick A. Stokes & Brother, New York, USA, 1888.

Chapter III:

Taken from *Histoire de la Turquie* by Alphonse Marie Louis de Lamartine, pp. 276–280. Originally published by Victor Licou, Paris, France, 1855.

Chapter IV:

Taken from *Mohammed: The Man And His Faith* by Tor Andrae, pp. 11–12, 173–186. (Tor Andrae 1936, translated by Theophil Menzel

1960). Originally published by Harper Torchbooks, New York, USA, 1960. Reprinted by permission of Cengage, Hampshire, UK, 2010, on behalf of HarperCollins.

Chapter V:

Taken from *Muhammad: Prophet and Statesman* by W. Montgomery Watt, pp. 229–240. Originally published by Oxford Paperbacks, Oxford, UK, 1964. Reprinted by permission of Oxford University Press, Oxford, UK, 2010.

Chapter VI:

Taken from *History of the Arabs: From the Earliest Times to the Present* 6th Edition by Philip K. Hitti, pp. 111–122. Originally published by Macmillan, 1956. Reprinted by permission of Palgrave Macmillan, Hampshire, UK, 2010.

Chapter VII:

Taken from *'Muhammad: Prophet of God' in Islam: The Straight Path*, 3rd Edition by John L. Esposito, pp. 5–17. Originally published by Oxford University Press, Oxford, UK, 1998. Reprinted by permission of Oxford University Press, Oxford, UK, 2010.

Chapter VIII:

Taken from *Muhammad in Islam: An Introduction* by Annemarie Schimmel, pp. 11–17. Originally published by State University of New York Press, Albany, NY, USA, 1992. Reprinted by permission of State University of New York Press, Albany, NY, USA, 2010.

Chapter IX:

Taken from *In Search of Muhammad* by Clinton Bennett, pp. 63–65, 229–243. Originally published by Cassell, 1998. Reprinted by permission of The Continuum International Publishing Group, London, UK, 2010.

Sources

Chapter X:

Taken from *The Prophet Muhammad: A Biography* by Barnaby Rogerson, pp. 4–5, 216–217. Originally published by Little Brown Books, London, UK, 2003. Reprinted by permission of Little Brown Book Group, London, UK, 2010.

Chapter XI:

Taken from *Muhammed, A Prophet For Our Time* by Karen Armstrong, pp. 16–20. Originally published by Harper Perennial, London, UK, 2006. Reprinted by permission of HarperCollins, London, UK, 2010.

The Birth of the Prophet:

Taken from *Poems of the Orient* 5th Edition by Bayard Taylor, pp. 105–110. Published by Ticknor & Fields, Boston, USA, 1854.